GOLF
FOR OF
THE FUN IT

GOLF
FOR THE FUN OF IT

Enjoy *Your* Game
No Matter What the Score

Michael HOLSTEIN
Scott ENGLISH

 MADRONE PRESS

Ashland, Oregon

For information, contact Permissions:

 Madrone Press LLC
228 West Street
Ashland, OR 97520

Madrone Press books may be purchased at quantity discounts for fundraising, educational, promotional,
and premium uses. Excerpts and special editions can also be created. Please contact Special Markets,
Madrone Press LLC, 228 West Street, Ashland, OR 97520. Telephone/fax (541) 482-8447.

First Edition

10   9   8   7   6   5   4   3   2   1

Holstein, Mike, 1942-
      Golf for the fun of it : enjoy your game no matter
what the score / by Michael Holstein and Scott English.
-- 1st ed.
      p. cm.
      Includes index.
      ISBN: 0-9704091-6-8

      1. Golf.   I. English, Scott.   II. Title.

GV965.H65 2001   796.352
                              QBI00-910

Disclaimer of Warranty and Limits of Liability
This book is intended as a general reference work, not as a substitute for independent
verification should circumstances warrant. Neither publisher nor authors are engaged in
providing athletic, medical, business, psychological, or legal advice. The publisher and authors
have taken care and diligence in preparing this book, but they make no warranties regarding research,
documentation, and recommendations contained herein. The publisher and authors disclaim any
liability for consequential or incidental damages springing from use of this book. They shall
have neither responsibility nor liability to any person or entity for any loss or
damages resulting from information contained in this book.

Cover design and interior design by Lightbourne © copyright 2001

Cover illustration by Jenny Anderson © copyright 2001

Edited by Teddy Kempster

DEDICATION

*We dedicate this book to the millions of
recreational golfers who play for pure enjoyment
and claim golf as their own regardless of score,
handicap, or level of accomplishment.*

*We offer this book to recreational golfers of
all ages, genders, and cultural heritages.*

We wish all who play a lifelong love of the game.

CONTENTS

ACKNOWLEDGMENTS

This is the part we really like. The book is finished and we get to remember and thank all the people who have given us the interviews, photographs, encouragement, advice, and the 1001 other things that authors need, or think they need. Without your help, we still could have written a book on golf, but certainly not this book. Thank you for your kindness, your encouragement, your expertise, and your generosity,

Jane Anderson, Jennie Anderson, Nadine Anglin, Peggy Atwood, Carea Baca, Todd Baker, Bob Beck, Vera Benedek, John Bloom, Gene Bowman, Dave Boyer, Darren Brogren, Brandy Carson, Carol A. Caruso, Tim Carver, Tom Doak, Wilson, Milly, Konrad, and Sharleen Chan, Jamie Cochran, Bill Cohen, John Cole, Jackie Daly, Judy Deggeller, Marty Deggeller, Mark Deggeller, Ron Dodson, Jennifer Donahoe, Donald Dunne, John Engh, Forrest English, Kent English, Donald English, Inge English, Joyce Foley (for the title!), Roger Foley, Terry Frost, Jimmy Garvin, Ralph Glenmore, Robert Glusic, Sidney Goldberg, Ken Gosling, Robert Graves, Roxanne Grubb, Jeffrey Gullikson, Daniel Hamnet, George Hannon, John Harbottle, Rick Hathaway, Christy Hernandez, August Hess, Barbara Hiura, Dorothy Hiura, Beth Hoffmann,

and Dedrick Holmes, Amara Holstein, Sandra Holstein, Seth Holstein, Sara Hume, Robert Hunt, Suzanne Huntzinger, Michael Hurdzan, Steve Hurly, Michael Hurly, Brian Hyun, Jerry Jakubczak, Carol Johnson, Bob Johnson, Mike Keiser, Jimmy Kidd, Wayne Kobayashi, Art Koskella, Steve Koskella, John Kremer, Byeong-Gweon Lee, Kike Linsday, Noah Linsday, Christy Mabry, Camille Matthiesen-Peryea, Cynthia Matthiesen-Peryea, Patrick McDonald, Carolyn Meyer, Ken Mickelson, Byunes Min, Mata Morgan, Jason Moss, Selma Moss, Adam Moss, Shanna Moss, Michael No, John Nosek, Patrick Oropallo,

and Billy Padgett, Jazzmin Parker, Kevin Patrick, Daniel Placencia, Dennis Powers, Taylin Rama, Robert Rankin, Edward Reed, Elizabeth Reid III, Harriet Rice,

Kristie Rich, Lloyd Rich, Nancy Richardson, Jeff Rigby, Mike Roberts, Gerralee Rothbard, Fumi Sakari, Ko Sakari, Masako Sakari, Perry Scanlon, Herman Schmeling, Wayne Schumacher, Trudy Scott, Levy Scott, Hanna Seltzer, William Shakespeare, Robert Sharp, Cathy Shaw, Saundra Sheffer, Jean Sheldon, Robert Sheldon, Fahad Sideat, Charlotte Skibinski, Isaac Skibinski, Adam Skibinski, Michael Skibinski, Phil Smedley, Noble Smith, Randy Smith, Winnie Stanford, Paul Steinbroner, Al Stetz, Dave Taylor, Erin Thompson, John Tredway, Robert Unden, Nancy Unden, Damon Vanderlind, Eric Watkins, David Werschkul, Hannah Werschkul, Jacquelyn Woods, Ted Wright, Aven Wright-McIntosh, Patrick Yates,

and we owe a special thank you to David Werschkul, our captain and mentor, to John R. Cullenton, Jr., our able indexer and the people at Lightbourne: Shannon Bodie who created the cover and interior design, with assistance from Bob Swingle and Gaelyn Larrick, and Teddy Kempster, our editor, who smiled a lot and understood what we were up to from the beginning,

and, truth be told, we want to thank each other for staying with a project much more complicated than we ever imagined at its outset, for learning by going where we had to go, and for writing a book just for the fun of it.

Mike and Scott

The Saturday Evening POST

July 26, 1952 — 15¢

Unsolved Mystery of the Air Lines
THE JUNGLE CRASH OF FLIGHT 202

The Great Lakes Go on a Rampage
By HAROLD TITUS

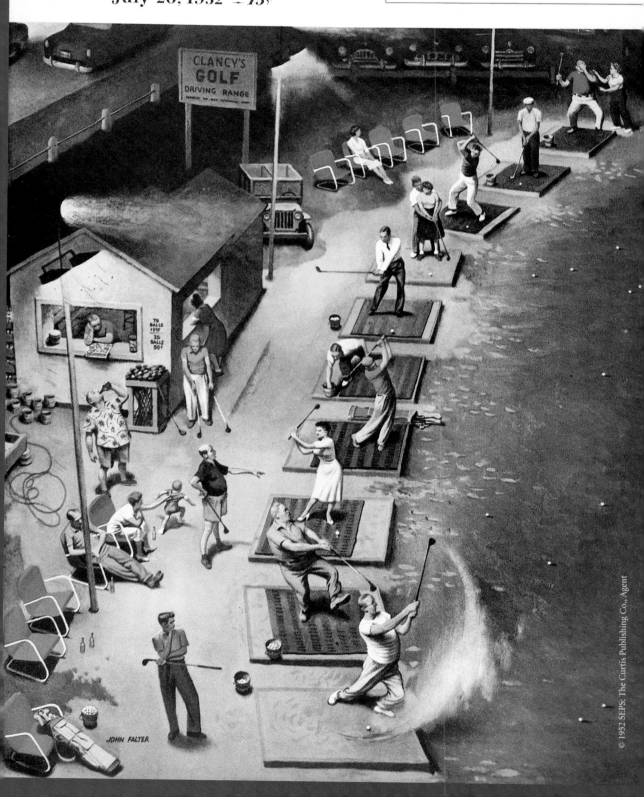

INTRODUCTION

Over every clubhouse door,
engrave these words:

*"Enjoy your game,
no matter what the score."*

olf for the Fun of It redefines golfing success. We abandon the conventional idea that a good round of golf means scoring well. Instead, we believe that the primary reasons for playing are enjoyment, satisfaction, and personal growth. To get there, we are willing to subordinate, even eliminate, the usual goals—low score, competition, and winning.

This book is different from many other books on the sport. It is about the *pleasures* of the game, rather than about improving technical skills, the best courses, or the great golfers. In it you'll find many practical tips about how you can increase your enjoyment of golf. These tips have nothing to do with driving farther and putting better. They have everything to do with appreciating the game, no matter whether you hit banana slices and duck hooks or crisp, accurate irons and long, booming drives.

"A couple of years ago I got really good. Played over 100 rounds during the summer. But the better I got the less I enjoyed it."
—Tom T., a member of a foursome we played with

WHO SHOULD READ THIS BOOK

In writing *Golf for the Fun of It*, we had you in mind if you are:

1) a golfer's mate, partner, relative, or friend. Help your golfer become a more satisfied player who enjoys every round, no matter what the score on the scorecard.

2) a beginning or returning golfer. We explain how to maximize your enjoyment of the game at whatever level you play.

3) an occasional golfer. Do you play once a week—maybe? We encourage you to take pride and delight in your game however often you get out to the course.

4) a serious or expert golfer. Are you getting maximum enjoyment from your game? Does a bad round result in lost sleep and "golfer's hangover" when you feel depressed for days about your last game? We'll help you add value to your scoring game.

5) a golf coach or teaching pro. This book will help you inspire your student athletes or clients with a lifelong love of the game and an appreciation of all its benefits.

6) an activity director or wellness coordinator. This resource will help you encourage people to adopt golf as a healthful, recreational sports activity.

7) a non-golfer. Thinking about taking up the game? We've described the many benefits of playing this great sport. Never say, "I don't play golf." Say instead, "I don't play golf yet." (What are you waiting for?)

WHAT IS RECREATIONAL GOLF?

"Recreational golf" means no-stress golf played during a relaxing, diverting, agreeable round. It means being away from work, delighting in the company of others, and enjoying big bone, large muscle movements in a glorious outdoor setting. Appreciating the details of play, our surroundings, our playing partners, and ourselves as we play is no small part of recreational golf. It can involve competition or scoring better, but it doesn't have to.

"Remember, it's called 'playing golf,' not 'working golf.'"
    —Peggy Atwood, LPGA Pro

Although recreational golf usually refers to actually playing the game, it can also mean reading about golf, watching golf on television, going to tournaments, thinking about the game, and talking about it. We are continually surprised at the unexpected ways in which the sport is enjoyed.

Lily, Scott's golf-loving golden retriever

Golfing friendships can last a lifetime.

"We have had pastimes here and pleasant game."
—Shakespeare, *Love's Labours Lost*

RETHINKING THE GAME

What are reasonable goals for occasional golfers, given the fact that the overwhelming majority of us don't shoot a low score? One is getting out on the course regularly, or at least occasionally. Another is enjoying ourselves once we're out there.

A third is to make sure that every time we come off the course, no matter what our score, we can say, "Hey, I had a good game today. I really enjoyed myself." The challenge may be to rethink what "playing golf well" means. It does not have to mean just breaking par or shooting below our handicap. When a "good golf game" can include every good thing that happens during play, not just the sum of birdies, pars, bogies, etc., we are on our way to playing better golf.

In the game we have in mind, satisfaction comes from companionship, the beauty of the course, the heft of the club, the moment of relaxed patience before starting the swing, the arc of the swing, the flight of the ball, and the sound of the ball falling into the cup. Golf can teach patience, self-control, sociability, and respect for nature. Can it also lead us to eudemonia, the philosopher's ultimate happiness? For a few moments, at least? Absolutely.

"Golf and sex are the only things you can enjoy without being good at them."
—Jimmy Demaret, *Golf: Great Thoughts on the Grand Game*

Play the game, really *play* the game for all it and you are worth, on your terms. If this means playing a frozen course in early winter, when the cups are pulled and no flags fly, so be it. If this means jogging while you play, that's okay. If this means playing with your children or grandchildren, so much the

The pleasures of winter golf

better. Celebrate the many games of golf.

Take personal possession of the game. Golf becomes surprisingly generous to those who ready themselves for its gifts. Golf is so much more than an 18-hole score. We all should feel encouraged to continually reinvent the game as our needs and abilities change. We've often felt that there's no better thing to do and no better place to be than on a course playing golf. We've written *Golf for the Fun of It* to awaken in all who play the joyful spirit of the game.

WHO ARE WE TO TELL YOU?

Disclaimer: We are not golf professionals, not in the usual sense. You would know this if you saw us play. So we want to tell you up front that we are in no way qualified to give you tips about improving the technical elements of your game. If any have crept

in, disregard them. We are serious *recreational* golfers, amateurs who love the game and want to share all the ways people have devised to enjoy it. Actually, this book would have been available sooner but we were constantly wandering out to a course to "conduct a little more research."

About Scott English

Scott has been playing for only a couple of years. His Uncle Don gave him his first set of golf clubs in 1998, old Wilson X-31 blades. The parish priest had blessed them, but I remind Scott that Billy Graham said the only time God did not answer his prayers was on the golf course. Scott learned to play with those clubs, then passed them to his brother David to learn with, so they continue to be part of the English family golfing legacy. Scott says that he tries to honor his uncle's clubs by

A joyful spirit

*The driving range where
we honed our skills*

introduced species. I see a bird up in the sky; he sees a raptor. Its wing-to-body ratio and deep, powerful wing beats tell him it's an eagle and not a mere hawk. Playing with a biologist gives a whole new meaning to the words "birdie" and "eagle."

Scott believes that golf courses, if managed properly, become useful refuges for wildlife. Professionally, he helps design courses by taking degraded landscapes and turning them into wetlands, ponds, and flowing streams and integrating them as part of the golf course. In doing so, he enhances the land for fish and wildlife habitat and promotes environmental conservation.

enjoying himself and introducing others to the game. He certainly succeeded in reintroducing *me* to golf.

Scott is our soils, wildlife, and water expert. Attracted to golf because it is an outdoor sport and healthy exercise, he says it connects him to the natural world. Scott enjoys meeting new people on the course. He appreciates golf course architecture, especially courses that are "discovered as they lie." He also enjoys playing courses in the wind and rain and loves to travel to find new and different golfing adventures.

Scott's training as a biologist has contributed to his appreciation of the beauty and natural setting of the game. He reminds me that the geese on the fairway don't know it's a golf course. They see it as a landing zone in their annual migrations. If I hit a tree, Scott can tell me whether it's a native or

Scott's encouragement to beginners

Since Scott is experienced at being a beginning golfer, here are his encouraging words to others thinking about taking up the game or just starting to play:

1) Hit some balls at the driving range just to feel what it's like. You'll be hooked.
2) Don't get angry or disheartened. Focus on your good shots. They'll keep you coming back.
3) Get lessons from a pro. Learn to hit the ball in the air, then hit it down the fairway, then give it distance. Up, straight, and far, in that order.
4) Don't go onto a course until you have a reasonable degree of control. Play when it is least crowded. Start at a par-3 "executive course" that is shorter and easier.

5) Rent clubs at the course (call ahead) or borrow a set from a relative or friend. Get professional advice before you buy clubs. Be sure you actually like golf before you buy expensive clubs.

6) Play with sympathetic, patient partners who remember what it's like to learn.

Welcome to the game!

"A fellow teacher was giving a group lesson to beginners. After several hours of range instruction, one of the students hit what was for her an unusually good drive. She exclaimed, "I hit a rider." "What's a rider?" I asked. "That's when it's long enough that I get to ride in the cart instead of walk."
— Peggy Atwood

About Mike Holstein

When I was 12, a friend taught me the game, and we played on the nine-hole Studebaker Municipal Golf Course in South Bend, Indiana. There were only two par-4 holes, we teed off doormats, and the sweet smell of DDT perfumed the morning air. There, I learned to play industrial-strength golf where the real challenge during a round was to find as many balls as I lost. I was a ball hawk, walking the roughs to find balls with fewer cuts in them than the one I was playing.

After I started, my father told me that he used to play. One day he found an old set of clubs in the garage and said, "Let's go and play a round." After that, we regularly played a little nine-hole course carved out of a Southern Michigan apple orchard. I still carry a black, delta-shaped chipping iron, my dad's favorite club.

I loved to play so much that I took a night job one summer as a grounds crew member at the area's premier country club. I ate four double bologna sandwiches to keep my energy level high enough to outrun neighborhood dogs that roamed the course at night. But it was worth it. Employees could play for free on Thursday afternoons.

Studebaker Municipal Golf Course

After playing the game sporadically in graduate school while getting my Ph.D., I finally gave it up when as a college professor I thought, "I don't have the time," one of the most common reasons for not playing golf.

After more than 30 years away from the game, I have rediscovered golf. Scott had a couple of clubs in his car and asked me to hit some balls, and it all came back. Golf *is* a wonderful game. Now, when I have a game coming up, I go into the back yard and start swinging a club. I take divots. About midsummer, the yard looks like some over-caffeinated gopher has been taking little bites out of the lawn.

Mike's encouragement to returning golfers

If you too have been away from the game for a year or decade or more, here are some of the things I've found to jump start the golf engine:

1) Before you resume playing, do some stretching warm-ups, then some half swings of the club. Go to the practice range, start with a 9-iron, and take half swings to get the ball up into the air. Gradually move to three-quarter swings, then full swings.

2) Don't be dismayed after shooting 120 or more the first time. Concentrate on making contact each time. Pick up after eight strokes (a score we call a "snowman") and go to the next hole.

3) Enjoy your surroundings and the great feeling of being outdoors.

4) Remember, practice doesn't make perfect, it makes permanent. Good practice makes perfect, so get some lessons from a teaching pro, then practice what you've learned.

5) Be more attentive to the details of the game the second time around. You will notice the fine points of grip, stance, and swing.

6) Play with different partners until you find a group that fits your style.

Welcome back!

Note:

The voice you usually hear is Mike's, but Scott wrote most of chapters 5 and 6 and parts of 7 and 8. He did many of the interviews in Chapter 9, and he speaks up in other chapters as well. Besides being co-authors, we are golfing partners and good friends. We offer you this book and the joy of golf.

Your authors doing the strenuous research for this book

A PEOPLE'S
HISTORY OF GOLF

"Golf is used by people of every color, race, creed and temperament, in every climate. No recreation, apart from the simple contests of the river and field, has been so universal since the world began. There is no freemasonry like the freemasonry of golf. Our happy game has wound a bright cordon round the world and so does she play her part in the great evolution of general contentment."

—Henry Leach, *The Happy Golfer*

Because golf is technically such a difficult sport, a great number of resources have been developed to help us golfers improve our game. Books, magazines, instructional videos, golf schools, and televised tips and lessons offer to instruct us how to better our golfing skills.

In all these helpful technical resources, though, where's the part that says, "Go out, have a good time, quit worrying so much about your score"?

The many pleasures of the game have been obscured because of a contemporary, single-minded emphasis on technical skill and the promised land of lower scores.

For centuries people played and enjoyed the game without much equipment, in casual clothes, without many rules, and without keeping more of a score than who won the most holes. That game is still there, still pure, still rich with pleasure and possibility, waiting for us to rediscover it and claim it for our own.

WHERE'S RECREATIONAL GOLF?

There's not much reporting of recreational golf by the media. Newspaper sports pages mainly cover professional tournaments and give us better golfing tips. Advertising does a little more. A few local TV ads show families and couples playing on local courses. There are ads for golf vacations

*University
students
taking a
study break*

and getaway golf trips in golfing magazines. That's about it. But for the most part, where's recreational golf?

The experts who establish the handicap ratings for new courses tell us that the average 18-hole score for men is 97, 114 for women, 100 for everybody. That means most of us need more lessons, better equipment, more practice, better excuses, or lots of consoling. Or maybe what we need is just to rethink our game, who we really are, and why we are playing.

"If you want to play better golf, change your standards."
　　　—Anonymous

PEOPLE'S GOLF

History affirms that it's always been respectable to play golf for the fun of it. Golf began as a recreational sport. It did not begin at an exclusive country club, nor was it originally the preserve of professional athletes. The history of golf is liberating. Knowledge of its origins and development can guide us in

the kind of game we choose to play and the rewards we expect from it. When we look at the history of golf, its recreational core does speak out to us loud and clear.

"St. Andrews is drenched in golf. It reminds me of a Spanish town when bull-fighting is afoot. Every man, woman, and child seems to have a stake in the game. The butcher, the baker, and the candlestick-maker but finish their day's work to be off to the links, which dogs, children, and cyclists make their perpetual playground."
　　　—Peter Lawless, *The Golfer's Companion*

WE'RE PAGANS AND KOLFERS AT HEART

Although Scotland has claimed the honor of being the cradle of modern golf, in the British Isles it was really only a local version of many golf-like games played throughout Northern Europe, games in which a ball was hit with a club or a stick towards a target.

THE GOLF-STREAM

FLOWS ALONG THE EASTERN COAST OF SCOTLAND DURING THE SUMMER AND AUTUMN]

(Vide *Report of British Association—Section V.*)

When in Rome

Even before Caesar divided Gaul into three parts, Romans were using sticks to drive balls stuffed with feathers into holes. They called their game *paganica,* from the Latin word *paganus* meaning villager or rustic. The Romans may have borrowed the game from the rural people they first conquered and then settled among.

Since legionnaires were recruited from country people, it might be that as the Roman Empire expanded northwards through Europe, country lads serving in the Roman legions exported the game to the provinces. When the Empire collapsed in the fourth century A.D., people continued to play the game of their former conquerors, only with local modifications. We know that guests were hitting balls over English fields as part of the festivities at King Alfred's coronation in 872.

Northern migrations

Paganica probably gave rise to a series of sister games, variously called *cambuca* in England, *chole* in Belgium, *choulla* in Latin, and *choulle* in French. Choulle was a cross-country game in which an offensive team tried to strike a target in a predetermined number of strokes they had bid, while a defensive team tried to hit the game ball backwards or into hazards, keeping the offensive team from making their bid.

Dutch winter canal scene from Munsey's Magazine

(Hitting your opponent's ball into hazards is generally frowned on in golfing circles today.)

Historical reference is made to men, women, and children driving balls across harvested fields in autumn. Another related game the French played was called *pell mell* or *jeu de mail* in which players struck a ball with a club and aimed for stumps or hoops.

> **TIP:** To get a feel for the origins of golf and for good practice, take an empty bucket or hula-hoop out to a deserted field or beach. Try to hit balls into it using your pitching wedge or sand wedge.

The Dutch played a game called *het kolven* or *kolf* in which players used clubs to hit a ball at two posts, usually in an enclosed space or courtyard. (Our modern word "golf" may be derived from either the Dutch *kolven* or the German *kolbe*, both meaning "club.") They also

played it in churchyards and roads, using doors as targets. In the winter, they played on frozen canals and, rather than aiming at holes cut in the ice, which would have been quite foolish, shot for designated stumps, humps, and bumps.

Dutch writers refer to the game as early as the 1200s, and early Dutch paintings show men playing and children holding clubs and balls. The Irish too lay a claim to golf. A Celtic legend recounts a golf-like game, and an ancient Gaelic tale describes three foster brothers driving a ball with clubs.

An early golf-like game

Asian golf

It's clear that there are worldwide variants of the game. The Japanese rest their claim on a game called *dakyu* ("hit ball"), based on a ball and a club and dating from the Nara period (708-793). The Chinese were playing a game called *suigan*, defined as "a sport in which you hit a ball while walking," a game that looks suspiciously like golf. A scroll painting in the Shanghai Museum dating from the Ming Dynasty (1368-1644) depicts three ladies at court, holding a club, a ball on the ground near a hole, and two ladies-in-waiting "caddies" holding additional clubs.

"THE ROYAL AND ANCIENT GAME"

If the Scots didn't invent golf, they developed it, codified its rules, and carried their game with them around the world. Our modern game came from them. Where did the Scots get their big idea? Maybe at an early date those Roman legionnaires brought it north into the British Isles. Or maybe the Scots modified one of the golf-like games they brought back from Holland or Belgium, returning from the wool trade or from fighting the English on the continent. Or maybe the Scots (and the Chinese) independently devised a new, local variety of whack-a-ball-with-a-stick.

At any rate, Scottish players seem to have been the first to hit a round ball cross-country, without interference from other players, at a hole in the ground. Golf was probably played in Scotland at least as far back as the 15th century. For all these reasons, Scotland deserves to be called the birthplace of the game that we know today.

or in modern parlance, do not even think about playing games such as soccer or golf.

Needless to say, golf persisted, and in 1491 Parliament had to once again warn people away from golf, one of the "vnproffitable sportis." However, with the signing of a peace treaty with England in 1502 and the substitution of guns for bows, national defense was no longer a good reason to ban golf. Bow makers could now make clubs, and arrow makers ("fletchers") could now make balls stuffed with feathers. King James IV began playing golf himself, as did monarchs of the Stuart line for the next 186 years. James VI, who ordered and paid for "golf clubbis and ballis," designed a seven-hole course at Blackheath in London, and the game was eventually dubbed a "royal and ancient game."

This 18th-century caddy would have to wait more than a hundred years for the golf bag to be invented.

Golf grew in popularity to become the Scottish national sport. Knights and esquires played side by side with commoners. Geography helped democratize the sport. Because summer daylight lasts so long at Scottish latitudes, working people could play before or after work. So from the first, golf was played on public lands at the seaside, within easy access to many classes of people, not just the wealthy, titled, landed, and leisured. Golf was of, by, and for the people.

No golf allowed

Eventually, golf became so popular that it invited political and religious regulation. By 1457, King James II of Scotland felt that so many able-bodied men were taking up the diversionary game that they were neglecting the archery practice necessary for the defense of the kingdom. So Parliament decreed "that the fut bal ande the golf be vtterly cryt downe and nocht vsyt,"

While playing a round of golf, Mary Queen of Scots mourns her husband's death.

"Hard by, in the fields called the Links, the citizens of Edinburg divert themselves at a game called Golf . . . . you may see a multitude of all ranks, from the senator of justice to the lowest tradesman, mingled together, in their shirts, and following the balls with the utmost eagerness."
　　　—Tobias Smollett, *The Expedition of Humphrey Clinker*

GOLF SOCIAL CLUBS

Eventually, the loose associations of golfers organized themselves into golf clubs with clubhouses, officers, and competitions. Drinks and refreshments were served at little stands out on the course. Dining and drinking in a dry, warm clubhouse after a round of golf were among the perks of golf clubs.

> **TIP:** If you get a snack from the cart man or cart woman out on the course, don't forget to tip. A drink, a snack, or if you have the time, a meal with your partner(s) after a round continues a long golfing tradition. There's always a lot to talk about.

By 1744, golfers at St. Andrews in Scotland formed the Honourable Company of Edinburgh Golfers. The St. Andrews Society of Golfers, now known as the Royal and Ancient Golf Club of St. Andrews, was founded 10 years later.

The golfing club made distinct contributions that had lasting effects on the game. Before clubs, groups of golfers had made their own local rules, sometimes at variance with those of players from other locations. Primarily to encourage competitions among all

Courtesy John Harbottle

St. Andrews clubhouse and bridge

players, St. Andrews's golfers adopted standardized rules which greatly facilitated matches between clubs.

Modern golf

British expatriates carried their love of the sport with them to their colonies, founding clubs in Bombay, Calcutta, Bangkok, Shanghai, Hong Kong, Australia, and New Zealand. These were reserved exclusively for the expatriates; no locals allowed. British residents founded a golf club in Kobe, Japan, in 1903 and the Japanese established a course in Tokyo in 1914. The sport became very popular but, because of high land prices, it has continued to be very expensive in Japan.

Golf moved to colonial America sometime between the 17th and 18th centuries, but the earliest recorded reference is a newspaper ad for golf balls three years after the Declaration of Independence. The game did not catch on until late in the next century. A golf club was organized in West Virginia in 1884, but it was not successful. The first enduring club was established four years later in New York, the St. Andrews Golf Club of Yonkers. The game rapidly gained in popularity, and by the end of the 19th century, there were 1,000 courses in the United States.

"We borrowed golf from Scotland, as we borrowed whisky, not because it is Scottish, but because it is good."
—Horace G. Hutchinson,
A Gossip on Golf

STICKS AND STONES AND BALLS

The earliest stick and ball games required sturdy sticks and durable balls. Any material that was hard

Japanese golfers on first tee of Oshima Golf Course, circa 1915

Ad for revolutionary gutta percha golf ball

enough to withstand numerous blows and still keep its shape was used to fashion balls—stones, knotty portions of hardwoods, pounded leather. A very early version of a golf ball, the "featherie," was made out of a stitched bull hide covering stuffed with feathers, traditionally the amount of feathers that would fit into a man's top hat.

The featherie, however, didn't hold up well. The average golfer could hit it from 150 to 175 yards, but it got sodden in wet weather and could be easily cut with irons. It was difficult and time-consuming to make and, thus, expensive. As a result, only the nobility, gentry, and the upper middle class could buy new balls. Ordinary golfers had to be content with playing with second- or third-hand balls that were cut, out of round, or found.

Golf balls became more affordable after 1848 when a revolution in ball making drove down the price of balls. Using gutta percha, the dried gum of a Malaysian tree, a Scottish immigrant to the United States fashioned a hard, solid ball, the "guttie," that soared farther and lasted longer than its featherie predecessor. Best of all, it was a quarter to a fifth of the cost. And a cut, split, or lopsided guttie could be boiled, softened, and remolded into a good-as-new ball.

Cheaper balls attracted a more diverse following to golf. Workingmen's golf clubs were organized to give apprentices and laborers the same access to courses that the leisure classes enjoyed. Technological improvements also helped to popularize the game. The guttie withstood irons better than featheries, and gradually irons replaced many of the predominantly wooden clubs. Irons beat down the roughs, resulting in wider fairways which in

*A "New Woman" of 1896
claims her game.*

turn made the game easier to play for novice golfers.

Because the ball kept its round even when mishit, golf was easier to learn. More people took up the game and more courses were constructed to meet the demand. Steel-shafted clubs gradually replaced wooden-shafted ones. They could be mass-produced, making the game more affordable to more people.

TIP: Some golfing families go back four generations or more. An album with photos, outings, awards, and courses played is a great way to memorialize a family's participation in the sport. Passing down favorite clubs is another.

THE CHANGING FACE OF GOLF

Towards the end of the century, golf became even more popular with women. The Ladies Golf Union was founded in 1893 in England, hosting the first women's championship. One of the earliest courses in the United States, the links at Morristown, New Jersey, was founded exclusively for women, who found golf liberating, physically and socially.

"The field is open to us, and this new life of vigorous and healthy exercise is ours if we will but embrace it."
—Mrs. R. De Koven (1896)

Technological developments aided the growing popularity of the game among women. Besides improvements in the design of the ball, another factor contributing to the game's accessibility to women was the development of the nine-hole course and the par-3 course, which could be readily played by women and children.

The first quarter of the 20th century saw the number of organized clubs, mostly private, increase tenfold. But, during the Great Depression, some private clubs elected to open play to the public to raise funds lost when members could not keep up with their dues. Some, verging on bankruptcy, became public courses operated by county and municipal governments. Poor kids earned money caddying and learned the game by watching. One of our uncles said that's how he and his brothers learned to play, that and sneaking out onto the course after caddying a late round.

20TH-CENTURY GOLF

Golf in the 20th century has been shaped by four major influences: touring professionals, the "stars" of golf; competitive tournaments; country clubs; and the marketing and technological improvements of golfing equipment. Each of these areas has made distinct contributions to the game, but each partially eclipsed the full recreational potential of the sport. In the following pages, we use the phrases "Star Golf," "Golf, Esq.," and "Golf, Inc." as fictitious entities, our generic terms for historical influences in golf and the various "cultures" of golf that have prevailed in the last century and a half.

A typical golf social club of the early 20th century

Young Tom Morris, for a time the Tiger Woods of the 19th century

STAR GOLF

Since the early 1800s in Britain and a bit later in the United States, touring professionals, playing in competitive tournaments or giving exhibitions, popularized golf, bringing many people to the game. In the 1840s, competitions held by clubs drew increasingly larger numbers of spectators. As more and more people could take the train to watch championship matches and as the rail system reached farther northward into Scotland, more golfers could travel to even the remote courses.

At first, tournaments were largely amateur invitational club championships, but later, they became international championships that gained the public's eye. Especially in the United States, businesses began to sponsor tournaments and put up money prizes. After 1950, larger and larger money prizes attracted professional golfers and media attention. Well-publicized tournaments always stimulate interest in the game. People see great golf played in tournaments and want to try it themselves.

That's been good for the game. Tiger Woods is the latest star with a large following, a line that goes back to Nancy Lopez, Jack Nicklaus, Arnold Palmer, Mickey Wright, Ben Hogan, Sam Snead, Patty Berg, Babe Zaharias, Bobby Jones, Walter Hagen, Joyce Wethered, Francis Ouimet, and others.

"I just loosen my girdle and let the ball have it."
—Babe Zaharias

Unfortunately, stargazing has its downside. Professional golfers create impossible levels of golfing excellence

Courtesy Arnold Palmer and Jack Stohlman

Arnold Palmer, who with Jack Nicklaus
dominated professional golf in the
second half of the 20th century

Scotland, competitive golf was played on the basis of who won the most holes, the most points—so-called match play. In the United States, however, stroke play or total strokes per round was the scoring version that prevailed and has made us Americans even more score conscious.

"One of the regrettable trends of modern times is the decline of match play, following the pervasive example of the professional tournaments with their necessary emphasis on scores."
—Peter Doobereiner, *The Glorious World of Golf*

Golf is such a challenging game on many levels that it's not surprising that the desire to succeed, even excel in the sport, has such great attraction for

that we may try to attain. The reality is that most of us accept that we can't slam dunk a basketball, throw a 60-yard touchdown pass, or hit a baseball out of a major league park, but we may feel discouraged if we can't hit a golf ball 240 or more yards down the fairway or consistently sink six-foot putts. After all, the stars on the Golf Channel do it all the time.

We forget, or were never told, that the pros have hit literally a million or more practice shots to reach that level of play. The result is, we feel bad, swear, become depressed, or, worst of all, give up the game if we don't measure up to professional play.

Historically, low-score golf is a relatively recent version of the game. In

Peggy Atwood, Head Golf Professional
Quail Point Golf Course

golfers. A low handicap provides a quick and easy measure of athletic achievement. It gives boasting rights to the proud owners of low handicaps. Go online to a golfing chat group, and you will see participants list their low or respectable handicaps in their signature. Golfers in the United States especially like to keep track of score. Par and handicap present tangible measures of how well we score over time, that is, how "well" we play.

However, a low handicap and the models of golfing excellence that pros offer us can, for the average golfer, be demoralizing. Most of us have little hope of ever coming close to par, let alone enjoying a low handicap. Only about 20% of golfers score better than 90.

"I used to play golf. My brothers played and I learned it from them. Now, I've got enough stress in my life. I don't want to go out for this big competitive thing, then feel bad and beat myself up for the rest of the week for not playing better. Who needs it?"
—Laura Y., former golfer

Low-score golf is a prevailing assumption, rarely discussed and seldom questioned. It is certainly wholeheartedly endorsed by most of the sports writers who cover the game.

No fair, he's having fun

Here's an extreme example of the grip that score has on the game as the media reports it. In the 1999 British

*Tiger Woods, perhaps
the greatest golfer in history*

Open, Jean Van de Velde, a French player who had never won a major tournament, had a three-stroke lead on the last hole of regulation play. Instead of playing it safe, he took several risky shots that left him in a tie. Ultimately, he lost the playoff.

His 72nd-hole finish sent television commentators into a frenzy of disapproval. One broadcaster kept insisting how foolish Van de Velde's shot choices were. "Stupid" was the word used, to the assenting murmurs of his co-commentators. The next day, newspaper accounts used words like "blowup," "collapse," and "choke job" to describe the Frenchman's performance.

The day before, however, after his

third round and a seemingly command-ing lead, Van de Velde had said some-thing unusual for a professional: "It's the biggest tournament ever in the world and I'm leading. What can happen? I can lose it or I can win it. Either way, I'm having a good time. That's the main thing . . . I am going to have great fun at home with my friends, no matter what."

What is really noteworthy is not that a pro lost a big lead (there have been others, the great Ben Hogan among them), but that American sports reporters could not imagine what could have motivated him. His decision to try the big difficult shot, not the prudent shot, in order to have a good time was incomprehensible to the sportscasters. His business should have only been to win, not to have a good time. Where's this guy from, France?

Do I have to be perfect?

Today's media coverage of golf is entirely score-oriented. Professionalized, competitive, perfectionist—that's the popular image of golf. The sports media prominently feature scores. Televised golf tournaments, newspaper and magazine coverage of the profes-sional golf tours, and tabulations of scores and annual earnings in sports pages are daily reminders of the ideal of low-score golf. No wonder that those of us who want to play the game primarily for enjoyment sometimes feel intimi-dated, even discouraged.

We shouldn't be. Professional golf has little relation to the vast landscape of golf as the public plays it, especially

The American aristocracy and its game

since, as we've said, the vast majority of golfers shoot around 100. Most of us do not aspire to a professional career, a low handicap, or competitive play. We hope for, but do not expect, a good round, much like people who like to fish hope to catch a prizewinner. We want to enjoy ourselves on the golf course every time we play. For us, the challenge is not to be seduced by the siren songs of low-score golf we hear all around us. Low-score golf can impose an impossible ideal for the average golfer.

GOLF, ESQ.

American golf did not begin, like its European counterparts, on public lands played by ordinary people as well as the wealthy, titled, and landed gentry. A century ago, an elitist version of the game, let's call it "Golf, Esq.," was the principal kind of golf played in the United States. Golf developed as part of the pursuit of healthy, outdoor exercise like tennis, polo, bicycling, horse racing, trap shooting, and hunting. Golf, Esq. began on private estates and spread to health resorts, spas, and private country clubs, which built golf courses to offer another physical recreation to their health-conscious, well-to-do city patrons.

At some courses shirts with collars are still required.

"There are also many occasions when a chaperon is unnecessary! It is considered perfectly correct for a young girl to drive a motor by herself, or take a young man with her, if her family know and approve of him, for any short distance in the country. She may play golf, tennis, go to the Country Club, or Golf Club (if near by)."
—Emily Post, *Etiquette*, 1922

Historically, Golf, Esq. was much more class biased, sexist, and racist than golf is today. It was a privileged game predominantly for Anglo-Saxon Protestant males. All others—Jews, Catholics, Italians, Latinos, blacks, and women—were specifically excluded in many club charters. The quip was true: "golf" stood for "gentlemen only, ladies forbidden." Golf, Esq., because it was played on the courses of private clubs, constituted a social marker—membership in an upper class gained by either inherited money or newly earned wealth.

In an interview, Levelle O. Anderson told us how a few black people managed to play golf despite the racial barriers. He said that he got started in golf when he was a caddy during the 1920s at the Washington Golf and Country Club making 25 cents caddying for 18 holes. No blacks were allowed to play golf at the country club, so his father and some of his friends roughed out a crude two-hole course on a vacant cow pasture on the outskirts of Washington, D.C.

His father gave him a 2-iron, the only club he had, and he and his friends used this club for driving, iron shots, chipping, and putting. The two greens consisted of a roughly mowed (grazed) surface with a buried coffee can for a cup at each of the holes. The game was played from one hole to another and back and forth, and up and down. There were no green fees. Maintenance and fertilizer were provided courtesy of the cows. His family and friends were always welcomed on this course.

A country club offered wealthier classes a relaxing pastime spent outdoors in a beautiful setting. Courses tended to be expensively manicured from treetop to ground level as a reflection of the monied class that "belonged." Membership in a country club—like owning a luxury car, living in the best neighborhood, wearing fine clothes—was an indicator of status.

Levelle Anderson at Langston Public Golf Course, Washington, D.C.

TIP: For a hilarious glimpse of the differences between private club and "muni" golf, read Rick Reilly's novel, *Missing Links*, a modern golf classic.

Today, we owe to Golf, Esq. the tradition of a recreational sport where etiquette, friendship, and fun go together. Good manners, proper attire, and sociability were expected at the Golf, Esq. club and still influence the game today. (Shirts with collars and other dress restrictions are the rule on many private and semi-private courses.)

Knowing the rules and playing by them (e.g., not nudging the ball to improve one's lie), encouraging one's companions ("your third shot was great"), affability and congeniality—all are part of the general aura of good fellowship and sportsmanship which in Golf, Esq. have always been much more important than winning.

A golf club is a place to socialize, often combining golf with tennis, swimming, fine dining, and dancing. It offers easy access to tee times, lessons, and well-maintained courses, as well as business and social advantages. Club membership, however, does cost money, sometimes big money.

What is Golf, Esq. today? Currently, club membership is more affordable and available to more people, often the

cost of a two-week family vacation. To reach a larger clientele, many previously exclusive, private clubs now offer golf to the public as semi-private courses.

But to many non-golfers, unfortunately, golf suggests social snobbery and elitism. Golf played behind walls and fences, literal or figurative, still symbolizes the biases against full, democratic participation in the game. At some clubs, old prejudices run deep—women still may not hold full memberships and minorities may be unwelcome. Unfortunately, Golf, Esq. has often followed rather than led the evolution of a more participatory society.

GOLF, INC.

"Golf, Inc.," the profit-driven, highly visible sport we know today, has replaced Golf, Esq., the version of the game that prevailed in the United States until the middle of the last century. In the process, golf has changed from a sedate, low-profile amusement for the wealthy to a popular sport that is part of the sports entertainment industry. Today there are more than twice as many public courses (almost 10,000 in the United States) as private ones.

Why this great popularity? Besides the innate attractions of the sport, which are considerable, there are two reasons. First, golf is a popular spectator sport largely due to television coverage of professional tours. The second reason is the vast amount of money spent

Choose your favorite club.

advertising and promoting the game.

The way the game is thought of and played is a result of the highly commercialized, professionalized, and technologized version of golf. The good news is, advertising, media, and the professional tours have indeed succeeded in making golf more popular. The bad news is, at least from the point of view of the occasional golfer, equipment-centered golf has emphasized golf gear at the expense of its recreational benefits.

Golf, Inc. not only promotes and sells the corporate image of golf, but it also uses golf to market a host of goods and services. If we can afford them, they can make golf more enjoyable. Some products are directly related to the sport, but Golf, Inc. also gives us cradle-to-grave golf: for young children—day care at the more progressive courses; for older children—golf (and swimming, and tennis) lessons. For adults—golf equipment and clothes. And when the weather prevents play, there are always golf books, magazines, videos, and clinics. When we retire, golf vacations and homes on golf courses beckon.

Golf, Inc. and Star Golf often collaborate. The marketing of golf began early in the 20th century when golf equipment manufacturers imported talented European players to tour the country, give instruction and exhibitions, and, by the way, sell the company's products. Gradually, equipment manufacturers found that tournaments were more cost-effective. Communities, chambers of commerce, or charities put up most of the money and staff to run the tournaments. Golf companies would sponsor a few of the best golfers who would endorse their products.

Golf = big profits

Golf, Inc. is more democratic than Golf, Esq., if only because it is more market driven. It tries to reach the widest possible audience with golf magazines, golf sportswear, and televised tournaments, both men's and women's. It gives us the games televised on major networks and the 24-hour Golf Channel, and the international and major national tournaments on the Professional Golf Association, Ladies' Professional Golf Association, and Senior PGA tour circuits.

The media do their part. Newspapers, sports magazines, and the Internet keep us tuned in by bringing us the latest scores and breaking stories. Current statistics for tour players include detailed breakdowns of not only average scores, but driving distance and accuracy, greens hit in regulation, putting average, birdie average, number of holes per eagle, and sand-save percentages. Postings of current money winnings illustrate the considerable financial incentives for making the top of these lists.

Golf, Inc. also provides the corporate sponsorship that allows tour players to support themselves apart from any money winnings. Today's best golfers make much more by wearing corporate names and logos than they do from their tournament purses. Millions of dollars ride on commercial product endorsement by the game's stars.

Planned obsolescence

We don't want to minimize the good that Golf, Inc. has done for the game. It has brought more people to the game than ever would have played

under the aegis of Golf, Esq. It has yoked its marketing efforts to Star Golf to the mutual advantage of golf equipment manufacturers, golf service providers, and the golfing public. Televised golf tournaments have brought more amateur players to the game, and technological developments have put better equipment into their hands. Undeniably, more people play golf and play it better because of the product development and marketing of Golf, Inc.

> **TIP:** To afford golf, one fellow of modest means we know has a separate bank account for golf. He deposits $10 a week plus all the change he's collected during the week. He also accepts cash presents for holidays for his "mental health golf fund."

But there is a downside. Through both advertising and media coverage of professional tours, Golf, Inc. induces in us average golfers a nagging sense of the inferiority of our game. Whether this "feel bad" effect is deliberate or not, everywhere we recreational golfers look, we see the image of sublime golf. Models of perfection are always before us: a swing like butter, an exalted confidence, an unerring putter, and the course management skills of an infantry general.

Nowhere, however, do we see the work that brings perfection to the professional golfer, whose seeming ease of play makes the game look seductively simple. Nowhere do we see the thousands of hours of practice in all weather and under all conditions needed to bring our game to a professional level.

What is never evident in the sports coverage or advertising by Golf, Inc. is that very few of us enjoy the subtle physical endowments, the timing, the patience, the focus, the discipline, the powers of mental concentration, the financial backing, or the six-days-a-week, six-to-eight-hours-a-day practice and play to perfect our game and then maintain our superior level of play. That perfect swing is earned by an average of 10-20 years of dedicated

Duelling putters

practice and participation in numerous tournaments before a golfer reaches a competitive level.

GLADIATOR GOLF

High-level competitive golf, Gladiator Golf, is the Siamese twin of low-score golf. It focuses exclusively on winning. Low-score golf emphasizes technical excellence. Competitive golf emphasizes triumphing over an opponent. And Golf, Inc. puts up the prize money. True enough, competition can improve our level of play and sometimes enhance our enjoyment of the game. But excessive competitiveness has usurped, if not spoiled, the enjoyment of the game for many a player.

"It was 'funny' last weekend when I shot the 94—in the foursome the scores were 76, 94, 96 and 101. Over most of the holes the 76 was being very vocal, club throwing etc., almost walked off on hole 11 after a bad decision. The three hacks showed good sportsmanship, joked and had a good time."
—An e-mail from Dave W.

Competitiveness is distasteful to some would-be players, more often women than men. Golf is still strongly gendered. Only 22% of golfers are women, and it may be that

Courtesy Jennifer Donahoe

Shopping for clubs

women are put off by an over-emphasis on competition. Perhaps this will be remedied as more young women play golf in high school. We saw one father-daughter twosome come off the ninth green. The father said, "Honey, can we go home now?" The high-school-aged daughter replied, "Okay, Dad, just three more holes."

> **TIP:** If you want to play golf competitively, try match play. Whoever wins the most holes, wins. You keep track of the holes won, and you don't focus on total score. That way you aren't severely penalized for a 13 on a hole.

PSST! WANNA BUY A GAME?

So the reality is that tour golfers are professional sports entertainers who have refined their natural skills to a high degree by playing and practicing almost every day. Very few recreational golfers can hope to equal their game. Nevertheless, we ordinary players are persuaded we can approach the consistent level of low-score, professional play (even though rationally we know it's futile) by purchasing some of the myriad of golf products sold by Golf, Inc. Each year brings newly designed clubs, shafts engineered for perfect flex, and alloyed or composite heads weighted and sculpted for maximum distance and control. Bliss it is just to think about such clubs, but to *own* them is very heaven.

Equipment-centered golf can frustrate and inhibit both our participation in the sport and our enjoyment of it. If we feel compelled to keep up with the latest, expensive technological developments in club design, we either spend way too much money (club models change yearly) or feel self-conscious playing with our "out-of-date" equipment. Golfers of modest means may feel that golfing excellence is simply out of their financial range.

> **TIP:** Prioritize your golfing spending: When you start out, rent clubs or use hand-me-downs (or ups) or second-hand clubs. Or, like Mike, buy a full set of outdated clubs from your pro with a lesson thrown in. Then spend your money in this order: 1) lessons, 2) practice, 3) rounds of golf, 4) more lessons, 5) golf outings, 6) now, and only now, upgraded clubs (graphite shafts, perimeter-weighted irons, trimetal woods, anchovies, the works).

RECLAIM THE GAME!

Unfortunately, recreational golf is the best kept secret about the game today, not having the press, advertising dollars, or aristocratic tradition enjoyed by the versions of the game that prevailed in the 20th century. It's time to give recreational golf its due. The whole point of the game is to enjoy ourselves, as many of us as want to play, at all stages of our lives.

So, we should say a courteous "Thank you" to Star Golf, Golf, Esq., Golf, Inc., and Gladiator Golf, and then proceed to the first tee and reclaim the pleasures of the game *wherever they are found.* For the first four hundred years of the game in Scotland, and millennia before that elsewhere, golf was played without rules, tournaments, or counting strokes.

"Therefore a health to all that shot and miss'd."
—Shakespeare, *The Taming of the Shrew*

After all, let's remember that it was not until the mid-1700s that golf clubs were organized, clubhouses constructed, and competitive events sponsored. Star Golf/Golf, Inc./Low-score Golf may stand center stage for the present, but it is only the particular prejudice of our current era, not the definitive form of the game. We inherit and continue a long tradition of recreational golf every time we play our round. This is the game that has evolved out of a very distant past, and it continues to evolve. We are only its most recent practitioners, and we witness its continuing evolution during our generation. There are many places to play golf and many ways to play it. An old game calls anew to us.

2

W H Y G O L F ?

"The game is a noble one—its rewards are manifold. It gives occupation to many, and health and innocent enjoyment. It adds a means of companionship to family and to friends. It is an interesting revival from an historic past. It comes to us pregnant with memories, promissory of joy. A panacea for woes and worries both of mind and body; an unmixed blessing for which we can scarcely exaggerate our gratitude."

—Mrs. R. De Koven, *The New Woman and Golf Playing*

Some people play golf with tireless dedication. A woman in a supermarket checkout line told me about her golfing son-in-law: "Jack doesn't play very well, and he doesn't care. He plays every weekend. He can't stand being cooped up in an office all week and not getting out. He plays even if it rains."

Many other players share Jack's enthusiasm, if not his all-weather determination. The National Golf Foundation's web page states that in the U.S. more than 26 million people over 12 years of age play golf at least once a year. There are more than 16,000 courses in the U. S. and an estimated 1,700 additional courses were planned or under construction in 1998.

Golf will become even more popular in the future. Soon-to-retire baby boomers, with money and leisure, wait in the wings. Players like Tiger Woods and Notah Begay are attracting younger, more ethnically diverse players to golf, as are youth outreach programs such as The First Tee. That's great. Young golfers make lifetime golfers and keep the game alive. Besides, I don't want courses closing for lack of players when I'm in my golden years.

HOW DO I LOVE THEE? LET ME COUNT THE WAYS

To those of us who play regularly, the real surprise is that even more

Love of the game

round when she was 84. No surprise here. Modern seniors live longer, are more fit, and enjoy more active leisure time and disposable income than ever before in history. You can learn golf soon after you learn to walk, and you can play it as long as you remain at least partially ambulatory. Golf is indeed a sport for a lifetime.

Aging may diminish overall fitness, but you can remedy that by physical training or you can compensate by using caddies or carts. You can also choose offset irons, clubs with larger faces, more flexible and lighter shafts, and lightweight, comfortable shoes. As a golfer ages and hits the big booming tee shots less frequently, improving the short game can compensate for the loss of distance. Scott and I have played with more than a few older golfers who don't drive long but hit every fairway

people don't. Golf is spellbinding. Maddening. Addictive. Relaxing. Friendly. Fun. Here are some of the many rhymes and reasons for loving the game of golf.

A SPORT FOR A LIFETIME

We can vary our style of play to accommodate our abilities no matter whether we're young, middle-aged, or old. Scott bought a used set of men's clubs from an 85-year-old woman who wanted to give her vintage set of Pings a good home. She had played her last

A game for the young and young at heart

Courtesy Big Cedar Lodge

Resorts like Big Cedar Lodge in Missouri offer a comprehensive package of golf and other activities for the whole family.

and are deadly from 75 yards out. Over a lifetime, you may need to make certain concessions to the game without conceding the game itself.

GET AWAY FROM IT ALL

You can forget your problems when you are out on the course. Golf involves getting away from it all, literally, because you go outdoors, often far from residences and workplaces. For occasional golfers, the game breaks the pace and changes the schedule of life. New scenery can even make you feel that you have taken a short vacation.

From the minute you make a reservation, you can start looking forward to a round. There's a special pleasure in taking the trip to the course and leaving behind usual routines. You make a transition between the everyday world and the wide world of golf. Horizons change. A new pace begins and you can

feel a renewing rhythm in your body. You're doing something different, new. Re-creation.

It's been said that golf is a stressful game. Not so. If you're a recreational golfer, golf can be a stress reliever. It gets you outside, away from it all. The game is demanding enough that you really have to forget other things in order to concentrate on it. Maybe that's why so many doctors, lawyers, and others in type-A jobs like to get out and play. It's difficult to think about anything else when you're playing golf— not personal problems, not work, not the stock market. Instead you're thinking, "Let's see. If I move my left foot backward a little, maybe I won't hook the next shot."

"What sport shall we devise here in this garden,/To drive away the heavy thought of care?"
—Shakespeare, *Richard II*

*There is no other feeling quite like
watching your ball take off.*

"Higher still, and higher
    From the earth thou springest
Like a cloud of fire
    The blue deep thou wingest."

—P.B. Shelley, *To a Sky-Lark*

THE FINESSE GAME

And now let us all praise the short game, the "finesse game," that part of golf played from 100 yards out to the cup. It's like playing pool in a park. There's an exquisite challenge to aiming, hitting, following through, and sending the ball on its mission impossible. It takes concentration, precise movements, and small-muscle motor skills. The short game is like fine-tuning ourselves.

You can have engrossing conversations with golfers about which is better, hitting a long, straight drive or sinking a 30-foot putt. Frankly, I've found whichever I've done most recently to be the more satisfying.

TAKING FLIGHT

One of the biggest appeals of golf is getting the ball into the air. What an ego trip! Watching a ball you have just launched never ceases to be exhilarating. That's why so many of us golfers gaze in silent admiration and self-congratulation at a long, straight shot we have just hit. We take flight. We become the ball.

BODY AND SOUL

For those with indoor, nine-to-five jobs, the game provides some balance to life. Golf is enough work to engage our attention and enough play to be fun. Fresh air and springy turf reward us with every step. On a good day, you feel like Tigger bouncing along the course. No wonder golf improves and maintains physical and mental health.

It elevates the spirit and exercises the body.

Good exercise

Golf can require physical exertion, especially if you walk the course, carry your bag, or pull your cart. Swinging a club and hitting a ball can improve muscular strength, endurance, and flexibility. Walking improves our stamina and, especially if we wear heavy golf shoes, it strengthens the leg muscles. And walking—but you already know this—is one of the most heart-healthy exercises. A typical 18-hole course offers about five miles of walking.

"Above all, do not lose your desire to walk."
—Sören Kierkegaard

TIP: Walk, don't ride. If the course requires cart rental, alternate driving the cart and walking.

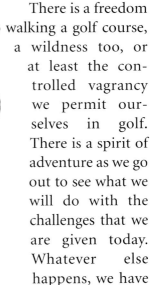

and workouts during the week, even occasional golf can promote physical conditioning. Like swimming, golf is an excellent long-bone, big-muscle-group activity. Just ask your doctor. If you walk instead of riding a cart, you get a gold star on your medical chart.

There is a freedom to walking a golf course, a wildness too, or at least the controlled vagrancy we permit ourselves in golf. There is a spirit of adventure as we go out to see what we will do with the challenges that we are given today. Whatever else happens, we have a good round just by walking a course.

True, the weekend golfer is not going to find much physical conditioning in one round per week, but if that round is accompanied by practice

"Golf is the exercise which is much used by the Gentlemen in Scotland.... A man would live ten years the longer for using this exercise once or twice a week."
—Dr. Benjamin Rush, 1779

Golfer's high

There are pure moments on a golf course, euphoric experiences when everything feels right. At the top of the back swing you just know you are going to hit a fine shot, and then you do. Maybe it's the power of positive thinking, but I think the subconscious is registering that everything—grip, stance, plane of the back swing, line—is perfect. A great shot has to be the result.

Sometimes, however, a feeling of absolute rightness flows from something other than the perfect shot. You are with people you like to be with, and time stands and waits. In the setting sun, each shot glows. You hear the music of the spheres as you wait for the morning fog to clear.

"Moon mist whitens a golf ground."
—Carl Sandburg, "Interior"

A good stretch prepares you for a good golfing experience.

Courtesy Simone Garlaund

OUT AND ABOUT

Where golf is played, the grass seems to grow thicker and greener than anywhere else. At the courses Scott and I usually play, we can see foothills and mountains. But I can remember playing on basically flat Midwestern courses that still had attractive water holes, tricky dog legs,

Courtesy Robert Glusic, wildernessvideo.com

A tree is 80% beauty, 20% hazard.

and some rolling land to enjoy. And there is always one flawless symmetrical tree, the kind you think only grows in garden books and seed catalogues. How can there help but be more sunshine, fresh air, and greenness in our thoughts?

Spacious skies and and wide horizons enlarge the boundaries of a golf course. As you move around the course, the wind blows, now at your back, now from the quarters, now in your face, or is still. Perspectives constantly change as you play. Just being out of doors improves your morale and makes you feel more alive. You feel part of a larger world. The sky brightens dramatically for the dawn golfer. The twilight golfer walks in lengthening shadows, feeling subtle shadings of the air as purple light changes into night.

> **TIP:** The best times to play during the dog days of summer are early morning hours or at twilight. Don't feel that you must play 9 or 18 holes. Why not 6 or 7 before work or 12 or 13 before dark, if the point is enjoying golf, not racking up an 18-hole total?

The dawn of a beautiful golfing day

Especially if you live in a city, where else can you find a place so large and so safe, so well watered and so green? And what a setting for walking. A golf course is part park, part garden, part arboretum, and part manicured lawn. The typical 18-hole course includes hundreds of acres. In today's world this is a wonderful resource, a vast, fertile playground on which to exercise our minds and bodies.

A PEOPLE GAME

Golf is a great excuse to see friends, colleagues, and family members on a regular basis, whether it is a usual weekend game or just hitting practice balls on a range. You get a sociable four or five hours to be together and talk. When you need to be alone, you can go out and play as a single if you choose the right tee time.

"Come, we will walk. There's other of our friends/Will greet us here anon."
—Shakespeare, *Measure for Measure*

With long walks or rides together in a cart, golf gives people who otherwise might have trouble communicating permission to talk to each other. Golf helps ground and ripen friendships. Some foursomes last longer than marriages, some until death do them part.

Golf is a great way to meet people, especially if you are new to an area, single, or retired. If you show up alone and are willing to practice until called, a starter will often pair you with a twosome or threesome. If the chemistry is right, you might be asked to play again and eventually become a regular partner. Or you might enjoy meeting and playing with new people each round.

Golf is also a good excuse to get to know people better. Playing with partners also develops social skills and good sportsmanship. Ask someone you have just met or someone you want to know better for a game. In relaxed, outdoor surroundings, you might get a different perspective on your playing partners.

You can always invite your companions to a driving range or the practice hole a few days before the round.

"My friend and I rent a cart and off we go. It's like a four-hour chat. We enjoy that as much as the golf."
—Shoshonna Slatkin

BUSINESS AND PLEASURE

Golf is a business asset. A golf course can be your outdoor office, a place to make business contacts, entertain customers and clients, have meetings, pay back business obligations, give perks to

Courtesy Robert Glusic, wildernessvideo.com

A beautiful, serene urban course—Family Golf Center, Chicago, Illinois

employees, and increase visibility for a company. Professional women are learning to play for this reason and are demanding entrance to formerly male-only clubs and changes in policies that restrict women's access to weekday and other less desirable tee times.

Business and professional people often use the golf course to repay favors and host clients. Golf offers a leisure activity in a beautiful outdoor setting, even though the clear purpose of the outing is eventually to transact business. What a job, you think. I can play while I work.

A golf course is also a place where people who intend to do business in the future can become better acquainted and feel more comfortable with each other. You really get to know someone when you are with him or her for several hours during a round of golf. Talking about family, hobbies, current events, even the game itself builds relationships. Deals may be made elsewhere, but golf paves the way.

Golf outings can also bring employees together and foster better relations. Company sponsored tournaments can team employees with customers and suppliers. Charity tournaments foster good will in the community and benefit deserving causes.

Courtesy Simone Garlaund

A family golf outing

"A few years ago when I was working on a difficult book project with several other authors and the project was past due and things were getting tense, we all went out to play 18 holes. We worked together much better after that."

—Ed H., friend of the authors

The family that plays together, stays together

Golf is one of the few games that children, parents, and grandparents can play together. During a tournament Scott and I teamed up with a father in his late 60s and a son in his 30s. The son said they played in all the tournaments they could find. "The only reason I play in these tournaments," he confided, " is so I can be with him."

A golf course is a place where husbands and wives can be alone, enjoying something together that has nothing to do with house, kids, or job. Even spouses who don't play can drive the cart or walk along. Who knows, the temptation to hit a ball might prove too great.

You can introduce kids to golf at an early age. Their pretzel-like flexibility enables them to do things adults can't. The combination of forward

tees and handicaps, either official or approximated, allows family members of different abilities to compete, though obviously competition need not even enter the picture.

A GAME OF SOLITAIRE

Even in a foursome, there are times we play alone, either literally because we hook our drive left and the drives of our playing partners are off to the right, or figuratively, separated by the natural pauses and silences that occur while others prepare to hit. These

Solitary golfer teeing off into the morning mist

friends, and co-workers by being alone, for an extended period, on a golf course. It's certainly an inexpensive therapy session.

"Although golf is a game played with other people, it is essentially an individualistic, and therefore a lonely, experience . . . a loneliness of endeavor often so intense as to be almost existential."
—David Morely, in *The Quotable Golfer*

TIP: During the day, you might be squeezed in between threesomes or foursomes if you assure the starter that you just want a leisurely round alone and will not be pushing groups ahead of you or playing through.

moments give rise to reflection and musings. Long walks to the green become opportunities for introspection. There is great pleasure sometimes to be had alone on a golf course.

When getting away from it all becomes essential, golf is an understanding silent partner. If you play as a single, you may have to play during off-peak hours, often at dawn or twilight. The reward, however, is four hours of sport in solitude, where consolation and renewal dwell. You become better equipped to deal with your family,

MEETING THE CHALLENGE

Golf is a simple game: follow a crooked path a crooked mile and get a ball into a series of cups along the way. But if you want to analyze the game, golf can be as complex as you need it to be. Consider the many equipment options. Multiply that by 37 flavors of grip, stance, swing, trajectory, and a hundred other variables that come into play out on the course, and you begin to see why understanding and perfecting their game are compelling goals for some golfers.

Golf offers a continual personal challenge. It is a test of concentration, physical skill, patience, and even luck. Some of us have played baseball, basketball, and football. Golf is different by an order of magnitude. If you hit a foul ball in golf, you have to play it. If you miss the basket in golf, you shoot until you make it. If you step out of bounds, that's a stroke and distance penalty. Ever-changing course conditions and the endless possible lies of the ball, combined with the vagaries of the swing, make every outing a new and challenging experience.

"My favorite shots are the practice swing and the conceded putt. The rest can never be mastered."
—Lord Robertson

You're the referee

In golf, you blow the whistle on yourself. Enforced by an honor system, golf rules require a measure of character and provide the chance to develop it. Because it offers so many opportunities to display honesty and sportsmanship, golf is a great way to teach kids the honor system. In golf, you're accountable to an absolute imperative: play fair as if the integrity of the sport depended on your fair play. And it does.

When the Scots gave us their national game and later formulated its rules, they included a Calvinistic opportunity to demonstrate moral excellence.

Even if occasional golfers do not know all the rules, we know enough to play by a general code that reminds us:

1) Don't improve your lie unless winter rules are in force.
2) Don't touch the sand before you hit out of that bunker.
3) Missed shots count.
4) There's a stroke and distance penalty for out of bounds and lost balls.
5) You can't touch your ball until you are on the green.
6) Before you pick your ball up on the green, you must mark it.

Do the difficult

It may *sound* easy—hit a ball into a cup in the least number of strokes—but the hole can be more than a quarter of a mile away from the tee. The cup is 4.25 inches across. The golf ball measures 1.68 inches in diameter. Thus, we must use a slender metal wand, weighted on one end, to coax a diminutive, dimpled ball into a preposterously small hole a long way off.

It takes a lot of physical skill to do this competently, and even pros say they can't do it consistently well. Not for nothing did Lewis Carroll call golf "a game in which one endeavors to control a ball with implements ill adapted for the purpose."

Some golfers are drawn to golf by its intellectual challenge. A hole may require careful deliberation because there is more than one route to the green. Do I play dangerously across the dogleg or take the longer, safer way to the green? Go over or under a tree? Lay up safely? Each shot requires that we assess the best route to the hole and choose the best club.

Competitive golf

Competitive play, friendly or fierce, enhances the game for some golfers. There are leagues, tournaments, and ongoing rivalries that give players the chance to test themselves against others. According to one poll, 30% of golfers say they would like to play in a tournament. And whether or not sides are chosen and wagers are made, there is usually an implicit, unstated challenge among golfing companions to shoot the lowest score, hit the longest drive, and one-putt the most greens.

"Near or far off, well won is still well shot." —Shakespeare, *King John*

This said, however, for the maximum enjoyment and satisfaction of *my* game, I need to manage my competitiveness carefully and consciously. I have to remember that recreational golf is not only about winning; in fact, it need not be about winning at all. For some occasions, in business and among family members, for example, competition should probably be minimized. If competitiveness ever turns mean-spirited, angry, or demoralizing, it's time to take a vacation from the game, give it up entirely, or go in for some attitude adjustment.

"A tolerable day, a tolerable green, a tolerable opponent supply, or ought to supply, all that any reasonably constituted human being should require in the way of entertainment."
—Bernard Darwin, *The Pleasures of Golf*

Adam and Hannah play competitive golf.

Golf has evolved two great inventions for enhancing competition: par and handicapping. Whether we play with other players or not, we are always challenged by par, the score an expert golfer can expect to make on any given hole. This silent opponent allows us to compete for excellence "against the house."

Cheered by a gallery of one

TIP: To relieve the subtle pressure exerted by par, average golfers can think of beating their "personal par," especially on their most difficult holes. "Personal par" is what *you* shoot on the hole on a good day.

Handicapping, giving strokes to equalize the score, is the great leveler that enables players of unequal abilities to compete. Parents and children, wives and husbands, men and women, old and young, beginning and experienced golfers can compete by adjusting their scores according to their handicaps.

The perfect shot

Once a hole, once a round, once a year, you will make a spectacular shot. That one magnificent shot will keep you coming back in search of others. Most golfers have at least a few good shots per round. Fewer have truly good holes, and very few, truly good rounds. But, ah, those perfect shots. To hole out a wedge shot from 35 yards or sink a 30-foot putt that calls "Clunk!" as it drops into the cup. Few things can equal this.

Golfing perfection can happen on the practice tee and even on the practice green. It did for me. One afternoon, disheartened at another round of pushed putts, pulled putts, short putts, and long, I decided to practice using a different stance. I started sinking putts. Three and four in a row, from six, eight, and ten feet. Sank them all. I heard a burst of applause from golfers who had been watching. I may never again be applauded for my shots, but this once I had the touch.

TIP: Just before you go to sleep, recall and savor the best shots of your latest round. You'll sleep better.

You will find it hard to forget the feeling of elation on hitting the *flawless* shot. Sometimes you know in your bones, even before you hit, that this swing will bring perfection. Such an experience unfolds in slow motion. You stand there almost hypnotized as the ball takes what seems like its predestined path to the green or cup. Whack, fly, bounce, bounce, bounce, roll, and it's in. Incredible! For this one moment, the skill of the professional golfer is yours. You smile and accept the hug from your caddy, the trophy, and the Master's green jacket.

"When I look on my life and try to decide out of what I have got the most pleasure, I have no doubt at all in saying that I have got more out of golf than anything else."
—Lord Brabazon

TIPS FOR BETTER RECREATIONAL GOLF:

Have fun.

Take it easy.

Take kids and spouses.

Play within your ability.

Watch your partner's ball.

Keep up with the pace of play.

Walk, don't ride, when possible.

Compliment others on their good shots.

Know where the toilets are out on the course.

Never be ashamed of your level of play.

Play enough golf, but not too much.

Notice your beautiful surroundings.

Control your competitive impulses.

Give advice only when asked.

Introduce others to the game.

Never become discouraged.

Be patient with beginners.

Know golf etiquette.

Keep cool.

Have fun.

A pro.

·LIFE·

FORE!
THE AMERICAN GIRL TO ALL THE WORLD.

YOUR INNER GAME

"Golf is a spiritual game. It's like Zen. You have to let your mind take over."
—Amy Alcott

It's been said that when you are ready to learn, a teacher will appear. Ready or not, Scott and I were fortunate to have several extraordinary teachers and teaching experiences out on the course. From them we learned that it's not what's on the card at the end of the day but what's been in the head and heart out on the course that makes a good round of golf. The quality of our consciousness matters most. That's what this chapter is about, how to increase your moment-to-moment awareness—your mindfulness—as you move around the course.

FIRST LESSONS

Here are a couple of the memorable learning moments that headed us in new directions:

Butterfly golf

The seventh hole at Oak Knoll Golf Course has its left side bordered by willows and a stream. It's a cool, shady oasis in late summer. I had hit a poor tee shot and chipped on from some distance away. It was late in the

A butterfly searches out the sweetness of the game.

Courtesy Audubon International

day, the light was a sepia shade, and I couldn't see my ball clearly.

As I walked up to the green, I couldn't believe what I saw—a large, gold and black monarch butterfly fanning its wings on the ball. The time of day, the quality of light, the ivory color of the ball—what a sight! There it was, Psyche, the Soul of Golf. I can't tell you anything else about the round, but I can close my eyes and call up the very image of that moment.

Goose golf

We were playing a high desert course just west of Klamath Falls, Oregon. Our foursome teed off first that morning when the fog hung so low over the fairways that we could only see the first 30 yards of our drives. Eventually the fog began to lift so we could follow a drive a hundred yards out, watch it disappear into the grey

ceiling, then see it drop, seemingly out of nowhere, from the clouds.

All of a sudden we heard a flock of Canadian geese circle over our heads and then fly off. We never saw them, but we heard them clearly. There must have been hundreds. The entire course was filled with flight updates, goose gossip, announcements, and tips about the best eating places at their next destination. Again, don't ask me what we scored that day. Ask me what a goose-filled sky sounds like to four mute golfers.

Rainy-day golf

We had taken our teen-aged sons to a day-long event about 250 miles north of us. All along the way, it had rained and the local courses were sodden. A pro told us to try the coast. When we got there, only two other cars were huddled together in the parking lot, and a 30-mile-an-hour wind drove light rain. Many of the holes had views of waves crashing on the beach, and the roar of the surf filled our ears.

Into the wind, our drives went all of 170 yards, with the wind 240, but who cared. The rain sank into the sand base immediately, and the bright green grass buoyed the ball up into an almost teed position for each shot. There was no reason to keep score. We just enjoyed the setting and every shot we hit.

Mentor

We were teeing up on the first hole when a single, about 75 years old, came up to us, introduced himself, and asked to play with us. He didn't hit long, but he hit straight, and he was *very* accurate from 75 yards out. When Scott asked if he wanted us to keep his score, he said he didn't worry about score. He tried to play at least five times a week, often with his wife walking with him. When she didn't want to, he joined up with another single or with a group at the practice green or on the first tee. He said it was a great way to meet new people, and most people he met this way he would want to play with again.

Later, Scott mentioned that this man played the kind of recreational game that he hoped to play at his age. But, we decided, why wait. We could play this kind of game anytime we wanted. All we had to do was let go of our overriding concern with "getting our handicaps down." All we had to do was stop being hypnotized by the number of strokes it took to get around and start noticing all the really remarkable things happening on the peripheries.

MIND MANAGEMENT SKILLS

Many teaching professionals recommend that along with our technical skills we develop good course management skills. Planning how to play a hole, which club to use, what landing area to shoot for, whether to choose a safer, longer routing or a risky, shorter routing—all these comprise an essential part of the strategic game.

Another set of collateral skills,

Rainy day golf

however, is necessary for the full enjoyment of the game. They include a positive outlook, mental alertness, and respect for oneself, one's playing companions, and others on the course, for the course itself, and for the game. These skills contribute to a mind set that prepares us to enjoy golf. They are *mind management skills.*

WHAT'S YOUR GOAL?

Efficient control of attention, taught by sports psychologists to improve the athletic quality of a competitive player's game, can also enhance the recreational side of golf. Here are some ways we've

A meditative moment

devised to improve our mental habits and enrich our golfing experience.

Think about your goals when you play. There are different kinds. We set *performance* goals for ourselves if we vow, "No three-putt greens." On the other hand, *outcome* goals sound like, "I'm going to win this tournament today" or "I really am going to break 92 today." But, most important are the *experiential* goals. These goals are about having fun, enhancing emotions, and having some private time to think, and getting to know friends or family. These goals are not measurable in terms of what we write on the scorecard. They are about what goes on in our minds.

GOAL SHIFTING

Why restrict our expectations to scoring well? Recreational golf is about all the rewards the game confers: getting away, relaxing, having fun, being with other people you like. It's about fresh air, exercise, and beautiful natural settings. Because it is self-refereed, golf even offers us the opportunity for ethical action and self-development.

"Golf is not about courses, handicaps, equipment or techniques. Golf is about what happens to you when you play."
    —Fred Shoemaker,
        Extraordinary Golf

It is true that competition can enhance our enjoyment of the game.

But for some golfers score fixation and competition overwhelm everything else. I remember a round I played on a beautiful course with spectacular scenic vistas that I never bothered to look at. They didn't register with me because I was concentrating only on getting from tee to cup in least number of strokes.

Diminishing the importance of competitive performance goals, or even eliminating them, allows us to discover the other pleasures golf offers. Here are some specific ways Scott and I have found to help us better approach the game.

COLD TURKEY: DON'T KEEP SCORE

If the pressure of scoring often spoils your round, just say "No" to keeping score. The next time you play, announce, "Oh, by the way, today I'm not keeping my score." Warning: You may be surprised how difficult it is to walk this talk. It takes will power, especially when everyone else is keeping score—including yours! Refocusing your attention will increase the pleasures of play.

> **TIP:** If you just have to have an 18-hole score at the end of your round, try this. Write down a score for each hole before you tee off. Now forget about keeping score, and go play your round.

Remember, many of us have been conditioned to think that good golf equals par golf and to concentrate only on beating the competition, whether it is other players, par, or our handicap. To suspend scoring seems to violate the purpose of the game. So expect some blank stares or ribbing from competitive playing partners. You might have to add, "I'm keeping mental score today," or "I'm playing this as a practice round" to soften the impact. At the very least, you'll get a puzzled look or two.

If you have a "score-is-everything" mindset, not keeping score may feel unnatural. Initially you might be hyper-vigilant and unintentionally keep mental count. Persevere. You have to bring a focus to your game and change deep-seated attitudes strongly reinforced by the dominant golf culture. This takes firm mind management. You have to decondition yourself from expecting rewards only from scoring well. Take heart. Lots of people don't keep count. Who knows, this practice might lead to your radically redefining your reasons for playing.

> **TIP:** As an alternative to "cold turkey," keep score until you have so many "bad" holes you can't possibly score well. Then forget about keeping score and enjoy the rest of the round. This practice is called "cool turkey."

The payoffs in no-score golf are considerable. If you face competitive pressures in the workplace, not keeping score allows you to escape from competition. Play golf to relax? What a novel concept to someone who plays everything to win.

No-score golf is also a good remedy for golf burnout, symptoms of which include a feeling that the game is getting stale and the old excitement is missing. Maybe a player has plateaued,

or is frustrated by "poor performance" or a feeling of monotony. Too many buckets of balls hit on the practice range have killed the joy of golf. In such cases, ignoring score may be the perfect way to discover other satisfactions in the sport.

BALL-BY-BALL GOLF

Another way of breaking addiction to score is to play ball-by-ball (B3) golf. In B3 golf, each shot has no past and no future. Each shot is a self-contained, unique event having no particular relationship to what has gone before or what comes next. Bracket each shot psychologically. Don't try to make up for mistakes on past holes. Every time you hit, focus only on the present shot.

In B3 golf, cultivate a joyful fatalism. Your ball lands in a divot? So what? Here's a wonderful opportunity to play a difficult lie. No need to ask partners, "Are we playing winter rules?" or worse, slyly nudge the ball out of the divot. The B3 golfer welcomes the challenge of each new lie.

Hole	1	2	3	4	5	6	7	8	9	Total
Blue	126	134	170	159	122	159	141	186	133	1330
White	95	114	145	110	102	131	110	146	102	1055
Red	73	79	85	83	75	108	65	120	86	774
Mike	O	O	O	O	O	O	O	O	O	O
Scott	O	O	O	O	O	O	O	O	O	O

Don't keep score.

"Do your best, one shot at a time and then move on. Remember that golf is just a game."
—Nancy Lopez

To get in the habit, treat each shot as a ritualized activity in which care and correctness, not outcome, become their own reward. The quality of preparation and ease of execution become equal partners with the shot you hit.

The approach. As you walk close to the ball, feel a combination of responsibility ("I hit it here; I must bear the consequences.") and absolute, disinterested objectivity ("In a golf cart wheel rut, how interesting!"). You are true to the spirit of golf. *You play it as it lies.*

The address. This, the most Zen-like moment in golf, helps clear the mind and lets you give the ball your complete, undivided attention. As you respectfully address the ball, channel all available energy into the moment. Take your stance deliberately, feeling each footstep into its appointed place. Hold the club, feeling the grip cradled across your palm, then protectively wrapped by your fingers. If you like to waggle the club, by all means waggle away.

The address

The swing. This self-contained, quintessential golfing action combines grace and effort. Enjoy it fully. Every golfer has a signature swing, an expressive outpouring of physique, personality, and character. For some, the swing is more acrobatic, for others, more balletic. Enjoy the human form in motion, your own and your playing companions.'

The swing

"There was the man who wielded his mid-iron like one killing snakes. There was the man who addressed his ball as if he were stroking a cat, the man who drove as if he were cracking a whip, the man who brooded over each shot like one whose heart is bowed down by bad news from home, and the man who scooped with his mashie as if he were ladling soup."
—P. G. Wodehouse, *The Heart of a Goof*

The impact. The moment of impact lasts a few thousandths of a second, but what stopwatch can measure the sheer thrill of feeling weight shift, hip torque, swing speed, and hope translated into contact with the ball? When you hit the "sweet spot," that perfect center of the club, you can hear the sound of perfection.

The flight. Many people like to watch the flight of a ball, golf's purest moment. When a golfer hits, there it is again, the momentary triumph over the weight of the world. Remember the featherie, the ancient ancestor of the modern ball? It was stuffed with bird feathers. That ball we just hit is our winged surrogate, and part of us takes flight with it.

The landing. This is the closure of each episode of B3 golf. What's required here is to mark the spot where the ball comes to rest and start walking. Take personal responsibility for the landing, feel your pride, resignation, personal challenge, whatever. You did it, only you. Then, until you next address the ball, the intervening time is yours to enjoy.

TIP: Best Hole Scoring: If you play a course frequently, keep track of your best score for each hole. That way you become less concerned with your total score for any particular round and more alert to those exceptional scores you make on individual holes. You can have an annual "best-hole" scorecard and a lifetime one.

THINK WHOLE GOLF

Think and act "whole golf." During and after a round, see beyond score. Undoubtedly you had a lot of good moments that had nothing to do with "perfect shots." Think back to the most

The landing

satisfying moments during your play. Look forward to those aspects of the game next time, and let them shape your expectations.

PLAY YOUR GAME YOUR WAY

Play the game that's best for you. What gives you the most satisfaction when you play? Shape the game to your own ends. What do you like and dislike about your game, where you play it, who you play it with? You paid your green fees, and as long as you don't slow play, damage the course, or disturb other players, you can depart from the conventions of competitive

The flight

play. Don't be trapped by a golfing routine. Question yourself. Question golf. Choose the kind of game you want to play.

> **TIP:** Sample different styles. One group takes their golf seriously. They know the rules, play by them, keep careful score, and seek to improve their performance. Another golfer says their group likes to mess around, talk on the tee, party on the green. Which group is right? Both are, if they are enjoying themselves.

Here's the cardinal rule for recreational golf: *play to enjoy the game.* Play different courses at different times of the day. Early morning and twilight golf give you different lighting, more wildlife, and fewer people.

Play at different times of the year. Spring and fall golf are entirely different from midsummer golf. We have played in fall rains and spring mists, and can attest that golf is fun in all but the most inclement weather. Actually, we hit the ball straighter in cooler weather because sweaters and jackets inhibit the big, wild summer swings that send our summer balls in such interesting

directions. Also, green fees are often lower in whatever qualifies as the shoulder seasons in your part of the country.

Find the right playing partners. It might be that those you usually play with are not quite right for you. One is too in-your-face competitive; Two gives too much unasked for advice; and Three drinks too much during and after the round. Who needs the aggravation? You might be more comfortable with other companions. Shop around. Form your own group from friends, colleagues, and family, or join groups at the course. You might have several different groups you play with.

Choose the right course. Do you want to be challenged by a course with long holes and difficult bunkers? Or are you more comfortable with a shorter, easier course? One of the best courses in our area has great greens, carefully cut and rolled, running true and consistent, but the holes are long, flat, and boring. Why have to hit a long iron or fairway wood after every par-4 drive?

> **TIP:** Vary the tees you play from. Hit from the back tees, the front tees, or mix tees up during a round.

GOLFER'S HIGH: PEAK PERFORMANCE

Recounting their greatest moments in sports, athletes often report feeling completely relaxed, in control, and supremely confident. They have an uncanny awareness of themselves and their surroundings, a feeling of union with the world. They experience time distortion (usually time seems to slow), an inner quiet, and an absolute calm.

The heartening thing is, we recreational golfers can also experience unforgettable moments as a result of our superior play—a chip holed from 35 yards out, a 40-foot putt that rolls in. True, a performance high happens a lot less frequently for us than for the professional or competitive golfer. We

play fewer rounds and are probably not as athletically gifted, but we can nonetheless be attuned to pride in our skill and feelings of personal triumph. When standing at the edge of a green, 40 feet from the flag, you just know you will make that chip. And in it goes.

"They would change their state/And situation with those dancing chips."
—Shakespeare, *Sonnet 127*

This event is not the same as *unexpectedly* making a shot. The dominant impression during peak performance is an unshakable confidence in the result, the feeling as you address the ball and while you are swinging that everything is so absolutely right, the shot must go in. So what if it happens only once a round, once a month, once a year? That feeling stays, whether we exult with a big "Yes!" jump up and down, strut around the green, or give a silent, knowing smile and feel the top of our heads come off.

"My husband and I were playing. I was getting frustrated because I couldn't get my ball up into the air. Then I hit a great shot. I gave a whoop and rode the club like a hobby horse. My husband said, 'Whoa. We don't do that here.' 'I do,' I said, 'when I hit a shot like that.'"
—Barbara H., weekend golfer

GOLFER'S HIGH: PEAK EXPERIENCE

The more usual "golfer's high" for us lesser mortals is not a peak performance but a peak experience, the main difference being that a peak experience can be triggered by something other than athletic achievement. Here are some accounts of peak experiences we have collected from other golfers.

Peak performance

"I feel great getting back to the course after I've been sick. Once I hurt my back bad and couldn't play for over a year. When I went out, I thought 'Wow, I'm still alive. Look how green the world is.'"

"Ever see the reflection of that mountain in the pond when it's perfectly still? Keeps me coming back."

"My son has emotional difficulties. It's hard for us to talk. Playing golf we sort of relax and open up. It's practically the only place we can talk together. Maybe that's why we both like playing."

"I want to be on the first tee when the sun comes up. I check the weekly sunrise/sunset table in the paper before I call in for our tee time."

Copyright, 1905, Frog in Your Throat Company

"You won't believe this but I hit close to that pond on purpose. I like to hear the frogs jumping in as I go by."

"The best time to be on the course is as the sun goes down. It gets cool and still, and you can see the world get darker by degrees. My husband and I love to be out on the course then."

"There's a course I play where a small herd of deer moves across the sixth fairway late in the afternoon during the spring. I'm not going to tell you where because I don't want a lot of folks scaring them off."

"Everything I look on seemeth green."
—Shakespeare, *The Taming of the Shrew*

GOLFER'S HIGH: FLOW

Like other human activities, golf has the power to totally absorb us. Hours go by like minutes. When we're in flow golf, "in the zone," the process takes over, and we feel a sense of effortless, continuous well being. A flow state, like a peak experience, is a natural high, and what flow lacks in the comparative intensity of a peak experience, it makes up in duration.

"I asked my partner what hole we were on and he said the 14th. I couldn't believe it. It felt like we had just teed off."
—Golfer overheard coming off 18th green

Flow is not about hitting perfect shots, or winning, or even having peak experiences, but about experiencing a feeling of being in absolutely the right place doing the best thing we could be doing. In the flow state, we feel energized and in control.

How to get into the flow state is the trick. Knowing about it helps. Flow can be trance-like. Thinking about it usually inhibits it. Just feel it. Having experienced flow in other situations—poker, cooking, shopping, even work, when you are really into the task at hand—you will recognize flow golf when it happens.

To activate flow golf, try the following:

Focus. When you are at the course, rinse your mind. Don't think about issues you left behind, the stock market, relationships, and health. Ready yourself for pure play.

Be aware. Pay attention to what's going on around you, all of it: the weather, the condition of the greens and fairways, your partners' personalities, your inner mood. Flow means being responsive to your entire environment.

Relax. From time to time during a round breathe deeply, take striding steps, look up at your surroundings and take it all in. Feel your body move around the course.

AWARENESS SKILLS: IMAGING

Imaging is a mental training tool taught by sports psychologists to coaches so they can enhance the performance of their athletes. It involves mentally creating the sensations of an experience, either before or after the experience itself. Athletes use imaging to visualize the specific skills they need. But you can use imaging in other ways to enhance the game.

Exercise 1: Club daydreams

Sometimes I think about each of the clubs in my bag. I think how I hit each one, how far I hit, what kind of stance I take, that sort of thing. Or I think about cleaning my clubs, taking

Courtesy Society of Golf Course Architects

In the flow of the game

them out, brushing the dirt out of the grooves with an old, wet toothbrush I use, and wiping off the club face.

Exercise 2: Swing daydreams

You can think about hitting the ball, the exquisite pleasure in the ritual relaxation of the address, the muscle tension and momentum of the swing, the shock of impact when clubface meets ball. Hear the satisfying sound of the ball on the sweet spot of the club that tells you the ball was well hit. Feel the impact along your wrists, arms, and shoulders. Picture that most satisfying of golfing sights, the outward arc of a ball.

Use the imaging technique to remember parts of your game in vivid sensory detail. This technique allows you to relive previous memorable moments during the off-season, midwinter, late night, or during illness or injury. Seeing yourself in your mind's eye on the course, doing well and enjoying yourself, that is a valuable mental resource.

You can also relive a round over drinks at the 19th hole. That's traditionally where playing partners share and compare shots, lies, and the lucky and unlucky breaks while the game is still vivid. The Scots invented the clubhouse so that they could have a place to drink, eat, and talk about their game. After your round, socialize with your golfing partners. The more we savor our rounds, the more we look forward to the next one.

YOU MUST REMEMBER THIS

Learn to recall your golf rounds in detail. Concentrate on specifics: the springiness of the second cut of rough around the first green; something your partner complimented you on; the play of wind on a water hazard. All these and more become possible subjects to recollect in tranquillity. Becoming aware of your round in all its rich detail—mindfulness—will add surprising value to your golf game.

Exercise 1: Your mental replay of the round

Mentally replay the round. In quiet moments, I sometimes like to rethink an entire round, shot by shot. It's not difficult, especially if I'm familiar with the course. I start thinking about the tee shot on the first hole and then mentally replay the round. Detailed visualization of a round is also a good cure for sleeplessness.

Exercise 2: Recall your favorite hole

In your mind's eye, walk your favorite hole and recall it in detail. Where are the trees, the traps, and the water?

What does the fairway grass feel like? The rough? The green? Think about what the hole looks like from tee to green. What do you see and hear when you walk down the left side of the fairway? The right side? The center? Think about walking your favorite holes on all the courses you play regularly.

Exercise 3: Remember your best shots

There is a particular pleasure in thinking about your best shots. Any golfer will hit several *better-than-average* shots in the course of a game—the gourmet shots of the round. Visualize them in slow motion, replay them several times, and then fast-forward to the next. Edit out the not-so-good shots when you do your own mental late-night sports roundup.

"Thou with an eagle art inspired then."
—Shakespeare, *King Henry VI*

TAKE OFF THE BLINDERS

A recreational golfer, unlike a professional or competitive golfer, deliberately cultivates "intentional distractions," that is, attentiveness to experiences not part of the golf game. This habit runs directly counter to the emphasis that sports psychologists place on an athlete's staying focused on the specific athletic challenges of the contest. Pro golfers try to filter out crowd noise, playing companions, all external stimuli that distract them from the competition. When he wants absolute concentration, Tiger Woods cups both hands at the bill of his cap. He channels his concentration on the shot before him. To lose concentration can be disastrous for the competitive golfer.

For the recreational player, however, taking off the blinders is fundamental. Deliberate enjoyment of the multiple pleasures of the game is our goal. So much the better if we are alert to the quality of the air, the temperature, the palette of colors on the earth and in the sky as the day progresses.

Even in a foursome, you have solitude and quiet. If you hit left and your partners hit right, you might have up to ten minutes walking by yourself during which you can meditate. Etiquette requires patient silence while others putt out. How often in everyday life do we enjoy opportunities for such calm, composed, and reflective moments? On a still day on a golf course you can hear

A picture of physical and mental health

the earth turning on its axis.

OPEN UP A LITTLE

What you notice and feel and think as you play may be of interest to those you are playing with. You should feel encouraged to share what you see and feel with your playing companions. Verbalizing the good parts will make you more aware of what exactly you are enjoying. Point things out to your partners, and they in turn will help you see more than you usually do. Scott is always finding red-tailed hawks' nests that I could never see alone. He knows which species of trees are planted along the fairway. That's one of the things I didn't even know I wanted to know.

The Careful. Brainy Player who holds up the field.

GREGARIOUS GOLF

"[A good match] is so fostered by companionship and wrapped about with the joys of friendship, that he who has his soul's friend for his golfing mate is on fortune's cap the very button."
—Henry E. Howland, *Golf*

Golf is so popular partly because it allows us to have fun with people in a relaxed, outdoor setting for extended periods. We are social animals, and golf gives us a good excuse to socialize. Couples, family, and friends can enjoy one another's company for hours.

PEOPLE WHO LIKE PEOPLE PLAY GOLF

Stand near the putting green just before tee time at a men's or women's league and you will hear laughter as golfers socialize before play begins. "Hey, here comes Mr. Golf. Just what color would you say that shirt of yours is?" In their voices you can hear the excitement of seeing friends and acquaintances again. The banter and jokes are infectious. You start catching the spirit of the game.

Even shy, quiet people become gregarious at the course. It's all about being with like-minded people who love to be together, outside, preparing themselves to play a challenging sport. Golf gives us the time to talk about social and political topics, family, personal issues, shots missed and made.

> **TIP:** Want to meet new people and make new friends? If you show up on off-peak hours as a single or twosome, it is fairly easy to get teamed up with a group or another twosome. Golfers expect to have others added to a group of less than four.

A FAMILY OUTING

The family that plays together, stays together. Playing golf gives family members a chance to enjoy each other's company outdoors. Many people

Courtesy Simone Garlaund

Family fun

introduced golf to their children and are still playing with them 30 or more years later.

Golfing spouses

Some women begin playing in order to be with their husbands. Enlightened courses now offer day care for parents with young children. For someone living in retirement, taking up golf might be the difference between sitting home alone or going out with a spouse.

"I got my wife to play by buying her a starter set. It stayed in the garage for two years. One day she said, 'I'm tired of looking at those damn clubs. I might as well try.' She loves it."
—40-something golfing spouse

Getting someone started may take some doing, but it's worth it. Golf offers a wonderful way for a couple to be together outdoors. But don't give a spouse advice unless you are asked. That's what lessons are for. Scott played with a husband/wife team. The husband gave a continual stream of advice to his wife. The only thing wrong with her game was her husband, and the worse his game got, the more advice he gave to her.

Bring the kids

Golf can be a wonderful family tradition. Parents can play with children, siblings with siblings, nieces with aunts. It's a fine way for adults to teach kids patience, self-control, and good sportsmanship. Once or twice a month my father left work early and took me out to play nine holes. Those days were memorable.

"Golf alone may lay claim to this unique and most important distinction . . . whole families enter heart and soul into the game."
—Hanson Hiss, *Golf Round and About the Quaker City*

A course owner told us about a 95-year-old golfer who has putting contests with the 5-year-old great, great granddaughter he taught to putt. In what other sport can there be a 90-year age difference between players? A putting green or miniature golf course is a good place to learn.

> **TIP:** One pro we know starts kids out hitting beach balls, then basket balls, then softballs, then tennis balls, and then the real thing.

Golf can promote family values. If you want to know about family-friendly courses and family golf vacations, go online or ask your club pro.

Although membership in a golf club can be expensive, if a husband and wife play more than twice a week, it might be worth while to join, if only as playing members. Some courses offer monthly or family rates as well. Membership gives you much easier access to tee times and better times on weekends, as well as access to the driving range and practice facility. Do the math. How many times do you have to play per year for the membership to pay off?

At a club, you get to play with other people who also play often. Children can get lessons and play along for free at more progressive cours-

es, so that golfing can easily become a regular family outing. Reciprocal arrangements with other clubs allow you play away from home.

> **TIP:** Don't carry a competitive edge out on the course with family. Play for fun, enjoy the day, listen to what your partners say. Family golf should involve no pressure, just good feelings.

Getting teenagers started is a special challenge. It might not be the parent, but a relative or friend who would be the better companion at first. Who taught/will teach your teen to drive? That could be an indicator of who should introduce your teen to golf.

Watching others play is half the fun.

GROUP GOLF

Golf offers a number of opportunities for group events. Courses can be reserved for a day if enough golfers sign up. Usually, a course can accommodate up to 144 golfers (4 teeing off, 4 waiting at the tee x 18 holes), but arranging fivesomes can increase participation. There are services that organize corporate golf outings, but it is possible to do it yourself with smaller numbers and on a smaller scale. Many golf courses facilitate group events, such as tournaments, banquets, and barbecues. The course pro or assistant pro can help you set up a golf outing, not only for work, but for church, schools, and other organizations. Just be certain to book the course well ahead of time.

Include a variety of events for people with different golfing skills. For people who want to learn the game, arrange a group lesson, followed by a mini-tourney at the practice green, chipping and putting at the practice hole, and maybe a trip to a par-3 hole late in the day as the "graduation" present.

A scramble (a group of players each hit, then play the best ball) is perfect for players of mixed abilities. If the group is large enough, you might want to combine a scramble for beginning and occasional golfers, and a stroke handicapped tournament (winner has the lowest score) for more experienced and competitive players. Arrange a barbecue or buffet after the golfing is done. It's always fun if someone takes Polaroids or a video that can be shown at the barbecue or the next group meeting.

BUSINESS GOLF

A lot of business is done on and off the golf course because of the relaxed, outdoor setting. When you play business golf, there are two possibilities: 1) actually doing business on the course, and 2) cultivating good relationships that facilitate doing

Combining business and pleasure

business. Sometimes you can do both, sometimes not. Just enjoy yourself.

Discussing business matters on the course is not always possible or desirable. Even though golf may seem to offer a wonderful opportunity to combine business with pleasure, be careful about how and when to mix the two. I once mentioned a business topic to a guest of our company during a round, and the reply was, "So, it's come down to business already, has it?" The tone of voice was unmistakable: "I'm here for golf, just golf." My partner took his game seriously and resented any non-golf interruptions. The game was his chance to get *away* from work.

On the other hand, partners may *expect* to get right down to business and respond positively to your initial overtures or open business topics themselves. It's prudent to get the ground rules straight from the outset. If you invite someone for business purposes, say, "Let's talk about this deal over a round of golf." Then everybody knows.

Be patient. Players need to get familiar with the course and the group before doing business. Let the game get under way before opening discussions.

If you invite a guest to do business, use the first several holes to socialize. Initiate topics of mutual interest—family, sports, politics, and, of course, golf. What are your common interests? Trade golf stories. During the middle holes, talk about business needs. Use the final holes to talk over how your business can answer your guest's needs. Discuss the particulars of the deal over drinks, dinner, or at a later meeting.

Another tactic is simply to play golf and entertain your business guests by showing them a good time. Transact the real business days or weeks later. Golf creates the good will and familiarity that encourage a good working relationship, which is as crucial to your purposes as actually doing business on the spot. If you are a good host or partner, you establish yourself as more than just a name or face. You become someone who is friendly, cordial, and a pleasure to be with. Every time you contact

Courtesy Medford, OR EWGA

Members of our local chapter of the Executive Women's Golf Association

your golfing companion, you can refer to your game together.

Women, business, and golf

As more and more women have entered professional and business careers, they have learned that golf offers distinct advantages. It gives people a place to make and cement professional contacts and do business. The Executive Women's Golf Association (www.ewga.com), a non-profit organization, furthers the interests of career-oriented women golfers. It has over 15,000 members in 97 chapters in the United States and Canada.

This Association helps women of all golfing abilities, offering lessons, beginners clinics, specific skills clinics, etiquette and rules clinics, leagues, outings, and other social, sporting, and professional events for women of all golfing abilities. It also sponsors a national championship series for accomplished golfers. Enhanced self-esteem, companionship, and networking opportunities are added bonuses for women who play golf for professional reasons.

Uh-oh. Playing with the boss

Here's the good news. You will get to know your boss better and vice-versa. This is your chance to look good. In fact, your boss might have invited you to assess how well you represent your company on the course. You are being looked at not for how well you play but how *congenially* you play. Are you ready to entertain clients?

The bad news is you could really screw up. You probably don't want to compete against your boss, especially if you are the better golfer. What's the point of trying to out-drive, out-pitch, and out-putt the boss? Just don't press. If you want to defuse the person-to-person competitive element, suggest a scramble. If it's just the two of you, try a two-person scramble trying to beat par. That gives a much more cooperative and less competitive tone to the round.

"A mark marvelous well shot, for they both did hit it."
    —Shakespeare, *Love's Labours Lost*

Golf with co-workers

Playing golf with co-workers is a great way to create good relations. Wandering around park-like acreage together, you are bound to bring part of that good feeling back to the work-place. You get to know people well and a special bond forms.

> **TIPS:** Whether with colleagues, the boss, or customers, be cool, play fair:
> 1) Don't nudge the ball or "forget" a stroke. Be absolutely honest. People remember.
> 2) Don't be drawn into a fierce competition. Your purpose is to create good relationships.
> 3) Watch your language, especially your jokes. You are representing your company.
> 4) Don't gloat, puff up, or get loud if your game is going well.

We saw a foursome of women at a municipal course. They had just gotten off work and were going to play a quick nine before they went home. One had started playing with her husband, she said, but that didn't work ("He was too bossy."), so she introduced her friends at work to the game. They play twice a week and don't let anything get in the way of their game.

FINDING PARTNERS

Once you begin playing, you might want to play with a number of different people. Maybe your "regular" partners aren't available, but you still want to play. It's worthwhile having a large circle of people to draw on, some of whom play regularly, others seldom. Here are a few methods of broadening your circle of golfing companions.

Pick-up games

One easy way to find partners is to call up a course and say you're a single in search of a tee time. They will match you with one or more golfers. Or just show up and tell the starter you are a single willing to play with others. You can wait at the practice range or the putting green. Many courses have public address systems and will call your name when you are partnered up.

"The friends you make on the golf course are the friends you make for life."   —Jessica Anderson Valentine

Leagues

If you are new in town or are looking for someone to play with, call around to the various courses and ask about their league play. Many courses sponsor twilight leagues, men's leagues, women's leagues, couples' leagues, senior leagues, and kids' leagues. If you want to try out the league, see whether you can register as a substitute. Then, whether or not you have been called, just be there when play starts. Chances are that someone will be a no-show and you will be able to play, sometimes for free (the green fee being paid by the no-show). Substituting gives you a chance to play with many golfers, and you just might be asked to stay on.

Golf leagues may rotate play on courses. Members expand their golf horizons by playing different courses and meeting new players with whom they may form regular groups.

Leagues offer many of the advantages of golf clubs (regular tee times, discounts for lessons, equipment, and green fees) without the expense of club membership.

Romantic golf

For sweethearts, a golf course can be a very romantic setting. Beautiful scenery, hours walking or riding together, fluid, graceful, muscular movements—what more could a person in love ask? A twenty-something told us that a golfing date "makes a great first date since the focus is on golf rather than on *us*." Besides, it's much better to say, "Honey, let's play some golf" than "Honey, I'm going golfing tomorrow."

Courtesy Charlotte, NC Chapter of American Singles Golf Association

A good way for single golfers to meet

The golf singles scene

Some golf organizations are open only to singles. The American Singles Golf Association is a non-profit recreational golf organization (they say their average member has a 25 handicap) whose goal is to bring over-21, single golfers together for golf, friendship, and social activities. "Social golf at its best," they claim. Go online (www.singlesgolf.com) or call courses in your area to find a golf association for singles, or get a local course pro to help you start one. Typically, such groups enjoy golfing together, playing different courses, dining together, getting group lessons, playing in tournaments, and participating in various other golf-related activities and outings.

Group lessons

Another way of finding partners is to take one or more lessons in a group. It's cheaper than individual lessons and a way to meet people. It gives you an opportunity to practice together, perhaps play with people you meet at the lesson, and maybe find playing partners. Teaching pros may encourage members of the group arrange to practice together between lessons. You can always organize trips to the practice range or play a round together.

Non-golfing partners

On many courses it is not necessary that every one on the course be playing, especially if play is not heavy. Find out course policy before you invite a non-golfing partner to walk the course or ride along in a cart. We sometimes see non-golfers with golfers, out for a walk and a talk. A non-playing companion is often an option. Just ask the person in the pro shop. Courses realize that guests may soon become golfers.

THE GAME OF "FOURSOMES"

British and Irish golfers regularly play a game called "foursomes" or "Scotch Foursomes." Europeans in general play more match play in which players or teams win holes rather than keep a stroke count. Many Europeans consider Americans far too total-score-conscious.

Foursomes is a game of two teams with two players on a team. Each team plays one ball and alternates shots until the ball is holed out or the hole is conceded. One partner tees off at the even holes, and the other at the odd.

This version of the game has been called the most sociable form of golf, an unselfish, companionable, team effort. You share the glory, you share the ignominy. To succeed, you have to know your partner's strengths and weaknesses and shape your shots accordingly. If your partner can't hit out of deep rough, for instance, avoid deep rough at all costs, even if it means hitting a shorter shot.

Foursomes is a faster version of the game, since one player sets up and hits as the other partner is moving down the rough parallel to the fairway, keeping a careful eye on the partner's ball. "Foursomes" takes anywhere from two to three and a half hours, so if you want a good, congenial game and have limited time, try it.

PARTNERS OF UNEQUAL ABILITIES

Some golfers, especially those who take their game very seriously, feel comfortable only playing with others of their own skill level. However, for most recreational golfers, we suspect, it doesn't matter. Scott and I have played enjoyable and instructive rounds with much more skilled golfers.

Players are usually welcome if they are pleasant, congenial companions, no matter what their ability. We once played with a fellow who hit a drive 30 yards into the rough, and the next two shots went about the same distance, still in the rough. He had a bad next hole too. Who cared? He was laughing and joking. He was a good companion. That's what counted.

For the recreational golfer who plays with partners of different ability, there is little reason to feel embarrassed or self-conscious about your level of play. If you want to play better, work on your game. Sure, if you miss the ball regularly, or hit big slices or bigger hooks, you probably need lessons and practice just to keep up your own morale. But if you don't have the time or interest to improve, enjoy the game you play. You are going to hit a few good shots. Remember those; forget the others. Enjoy the outing.

GOLF ETIQUETTE

Golf etiquette comprises the traditional, voluntary standards of behavior that regulate conduct on the course—the good golf behavior that makes the game enjoyable for everyone. Experienced players model good (or bad) behavior for less-experienced golfers, so we owe it to the game, other golfers, and ourselves to observe good golf etiquette. It is as important as any technical facet. It preserves the quality of the game.

Be quiet

The grip, stance, and swing require mental concentration, and golfers respect that need by not talking or moving when another player prepares to hit. That courtesy extends to golfers in other groups. For instance, we are expected to time our arrival at the next tee so that our cart and conversation do not distract a golfer teeing off.

'Forgive you?' he muttered. 'Can you forgive me? Me—a tee-talker, a green-gabbler, a prattler on the links, the lowest form of life known to science? I am unclean, unclean!'
—P.G. Wodehouse, *The Salvation of George MacKintosh*

Be quick

Golfers are expected to keep up with the flow of traffic on the course. Slow play is probably the worst breach of etiquette because it slows down everyone behind the slow players. Marshals ride around in carts and issue warnings or eject players for slow play.

If you want to play slowly, let the people behind you play through.

Stand to the side of the green and wave them on, putt out, and wait at the next tee for them to go ahead of you. Or play when the course is not so crowded and you can move at your more leisurely pace.

"And I shall here abide the hourly shot."
—Shakespeare, *Cymbeline*

Courtesy Simone Garlaund

Hoping the foursome ahead will pick up the pace

TIPS: To avoid slow play:

1) Take one practice swing while others are getting ready. When it's your turn, just hit the ball.

2) If you use a cart, choose your club and the next lower and higher ones too when you walk to your ball. At the green, park your cart (or pull cart) nearest the next tee.

3) If you are the passenger, get in, hold your club until you stop, then put it in your bag.

4) If a partner loses a ball, hit yours, and then help look. Chances are your partner will have already found the ball. If play is heavy, take a few minutes then drop a new ball.

5) Play "ready golf": whoever is ready hits next. Have shorter hitters tee off first.

6) Putt when ready and hole out. Stand near your ball so you're ready to putt.

7) Mark your scorecard well off the green on your way to the next tee.

8) Keep up with the foursome ahead of yours.

Be careful

On a golf course, a hard, small projectile is driven a long way with tremendous force. As Grandma used to say, "You can lose an eye doing that." A boy in my neighborhood did in fact lose an eye while caddying. He was standing slightly in front of a golfer who hit a drive off the toe of the club. Moral: always stand *behind* a hitter.

Wait until the golfers in the party ahead are well out of range before you hit. You don't want your career shot ruined by really hurting someone and prompting a lawsuit.

If you or a partner hit a ball towards someone, yell "Fore." If someone yells "Fore," crouch and cover your head. Don't worry about looking foolish. Getting a concussion after a warning would be foolish.

"But, as the Devil would have it, three misbegotten knaves in Kendal green came at my back and let drive at me."
—Shakespeare,
Henry IV, Part I

Club throwing is childish, unsportsmanlike, and dangerous. It should never be tolerated. If you witness it, say, "Club throwing is not acceptable. Don't do it." Club pounding is also dangerous. There is a story circulating of a golfer who, after a bad shot, pounded the offending iron against his bag. The head snapped off and severed his carotid artery. He died on the spot.

"Once in high school I skipped church to play golf. About 2 p.m. we got to the 18th hole, an unusual par 3 that played uphill. On the left of the fairway was the course restaurant, with a wall of glass that gave diners a view over the course. Protecting the glass

Out of control

was a large old tree. I hit my shot poorly and in a fit of pique, tossed my iron high in the air. It stuck in the branches of the tree. It was a good club. I could see it and decided to climb after it. As I reached the higher branches I became aware that I was eyeball-to-eyeball with the folks having lunch. Looking straight at me, with a not-so-forgiving glare, was the minister of our church. Haven't thrown a club since."

—Randy Smith

Cart safety dictates two occupants per cart and feet inside a moving cart.

Carts tip, so drive slowly on slopes, on wet grass, and when turning. If you see irresponsible behavior, note the time and hole and report it. A DUI citation can be issued on most municipal and some private courses for drunken cart driving. Report it. Do everyone a favor, the driver included.

Get off the course in a lightning storm. Golfers waving metal rods make easy targets. Once, we played the last four holes in a thunderstorm although all of us knew better. The risk/reward ratio was definitely not in our favor.

Be considerate

Out on the course you are at least temporarily "Owners of the Course." Exercise proprietary concern for the grounds. Don't litter. Repair any damage caused. The principle in golf, as in life, is leave the place better than you found it.

Good course stewardship goes beyond rectifying damage you do. Replace a divot or two in the fairway. Try to repair at least one other ball mark after you repair your own. Every golfer is part of a volunteer course maintenance squad. One unrepaired divot and one beer can on a fairway attract ten more, just as a broken window in a building invites more stones.

TIPS:

1) If you lift a divot (scoop out a grassy "scalp"), retrieve it, replace it, and tramp it down. (Certain grasses do not regenerate from replaced divots, so check at the pro shop.) Some courses have scoops and a mix of sand and grass seed for you to reseed divots.

2) Leave sand bunkers the way you would like to find them. This means entering from the lowest point closest to the ball, minimal walking, no practice swings into the sand (even touching sand with hand or club costs you a stroke), and raking footprints smooth.

3) Be careful on greens. Don't drag spiked shoes across the grass. Choose plastic, not metal spikes that damage turf. Or use treaded shoes that do less damage.

4) Hold the pin or drop it carefully. Don't throw it down; it can groove a green.

Be courteous

Traditionally, the player with the lowest score on the previous hole has the "honor" of teeing first on the next tee. The honor is kept until another player wins, not just ties, a hole. Stand out of the line of sight and peripheral vision of a golfer making a shot. Watch the line of flight of your and your playing partners' balls and note where they land so you will be able to find them quickly.

The player farthest from the hole putts first. Step over the imaginary lines connecting other players' balls with the hole. Don't let your shadow fall over the line to the hole when another player is putting. Wait until everyone putts out before you walk off the green.

If your ball is in the way, offer to mark it using a ball marker or dime (put the marker down behind your ball then pick up your ball). The closest player to the hole usually asks other players whether they want the pin tended or removed. ("Do you want it in or out?") If the answer is "in" or "tended," hold the flag stick in the hole and remove it after the ball is struck. Stand still and be quiet when others putt.

> **TIP:** Nod and smile at and greet people on the course. "How's it going?" or "Great day for golf." Like you, they are there to enjoy themselves. Be of good cheer and good will.

PROBLEM BEHAVIOR

It's been said that golf people are good people, but even good people can do bad things. If you see flagrant disregard of golf etiquette or safety, the issue becomes what to say and how to say it. Judgment and tact are needed. Is the problem serious enough to warrant comment?

Sometimes problematic behavior can continue or even spiral out of control. We have seen temper tantrums spread during a round. Someone hits a poor shot and slams the club into the bag; the next poor shot is rewarded with a curse; the next, a pounded club; later, a thrown club. With each escalation of anger, the pleasure of the game diminishes for all the playing partners.

One way of calling attention to the problem is using the "we" or "I" rather than the "you" pronoun. So it's, "We really need to keep up the pace today since the course is so crowded" as a way of handling a partner's slow play. Try, "I lose concentration when you swear" rather than "Hey, watch the language."

Or, "I sometimes forget to rake the trap after I miss a shot too." These are less confrontational than more direct methods. If your foursome agrees, tax expletives a dime, payable on the spot. (Dimes make good ball markers.)

THE RULES

The better or more serious about the game you become, the more important it is to play by the rules. Honesty is the ethos of golf. The challenge of golf is the difficult shot. Playing a buried lie out of a footprint in sand is what the game is all about. At a certain level of experience, one knows all the rules and plays by them. *Noblesse oblige.*

If you are establishing your handicap, you need to know things like when to assess yourself penalties, when you may and may not move the ball to give yourself relief from a hazard, and what to do with an out-of-bounds ball. In a tournament, you must know and play by the rules, so before you play, buy and study the rulebook and carry it with you in your bag.

Playing by the rules means "playing it down" or "playing it as it lies." No fluffing up the ball by rolling or nudging it into a better position. No conceding or accepting "gimmies" (short putts) in stroke play. Counting *all* the strokes you take. Accepting penalty strokes.

If you are a beginner, however, don't get too exercised over *the rules.* Your job is to get the ball in the air, down the fairway, and into the hole. It's even okay to tee the ball up in the fairway until your skill

The Golden Rule of Golf
(Our proposed addition to the USGA Rules of Golf)

Required Attitude

0-1 Play is to be guided by the principle
that the game of golf is a joy forever.

0-2 Whether in competitive or casual play, a player shall maintain
a demeanor that is friendly, congratulatory, and appreciative of
the game, the play, and playing partners.

0-3 Each game shall begin, continue, and end as the best of times, an epoch
of belief, a season of light, a spring of hope, and the confidence that,
standing on the first tee, we golfers do indeed have everything before us.

0-4 Enjoy your game no matter what the score.

---

improves. Most other players won't care. They are thinking about their own game. As you get better, you can push the tee farther into the ground. Then use no tee, but declare on the first tee, "I'm playing winter rules!" which means you can bump the ball into a better lie if you want. Eventually you won't need these crutches.

The etiquette in modifying the rules is to let your partners know from the first tee what you are doing and why. Say something like, "I haven't played recently, so it's 'winter rules' for me today, okay?" Get general agreement for any rule suspension. Say, "Is one mulligan per nine all right with everybody?" (A "mulligan" is a make-up shot that you don't have to count.) Otherwise, your partners think you don't know the rules, don't care, or are trying to trick them.

"A few strong instincts, and a few plain rules."
—William Wordsworth

MISSIONARIES OF THE GAME

Once we have enjoyed this wonderful game, it is natural to want to share it with others around us. Part of the fun of golf is talking about it. Anyone who plays has stories, theories, and best and worst rounds to share. Anyone who doesn't play knows someone who does. Your enthusiastic account of a golf round can bring people to the game. For those whose pleasure in the game includes a larger sense of mission, here are several ways to carry golf to more people. You may know of other efforts in your area.

1) Local courses can sponsor "community outreach" programs that offer introductory golf lesson packages, including reduced rates on lessons, equipment, and green fees.
2) Golf course tours can be offered to acquaint people with a course and the basic structure of the sport. An Audubon Christmas bird count can educate the public in the value of courses to wildlife.
3) Some courses have public access trails around the edges of the course; these paths are set aside for walking, jogging, cross-country training, bird watching and other activities.
4) Charity golf is an excellent way to expose the community to golf while raising money for charitable organizations and school functions.
5) We've heard of a "golf club library" based on the model of a lending library. Donated golf bags and clubs can be checked out at a clubhouse for free, but have to be returned. This policy gives people a chance to try out the game before investing in clubs.

Special needs equipment makes golf accessible to everyone.

Golfers with disabilities

The heritage of golf as a game for everyone has become even more realizable in the last decade or so. The Americans With Disabilities Act, passed in the United States in 1990, has accelerated accessibility to courses, resorts, and golfing establishments for people who are physically and mentally disabled. People with disabilities can take up the game; golfers with disabilities can play; and golfers who develop disabilities can continue to play.

Currently, a number of groups help facilitate access to golf. National and regional blind golf associations assist golfers who are blind, for example, the United States Blind Golf Association (www.blindgolf.com). (Golfers who are blind and visually impaired typically play with a coach who gives them the distance and direction of shots.) There

Courtesy Kevin Patrick; Dave Boyer photographer

is also a National Amputee Golf Association (www.amputee-golf.org) and The Association of Disabled Americans (www.adag.org).

A host of adjustments, adaptive services, and products enable golfers of all physical and mental abilities to play. Special carts provide access to courses for golfers who can't stand. Special clubs and fittings make it possible for amputees and golfers suffering from arthritis to grip a club. The USGA and Royal and Ancient Golf Club of St. Andrews, Scotland, have issued modifications of the rules of golf enabling golfers with disabilities to compete and maintain the integrity and spirit of competitive play.

That's all as it should be. It is right and proper that all persons who can play golf do have access to golf. Because many people with disabilities can take up or continue playing golf, that's good for golf. And, after all, able-bodied golf exists on a spectrum with assisted golf. Those of us who intend to play golf for a lifetime may well need to avail ourselves of assisted golf services and products at some time in our playing career.

Youth advocacy

Imagine an urban street corner where a group of kids with their golf bags are picked up by a taxi and taken to the local municipal course where they get free lessons from the pro and then play a free round. Outreach programs like this bring young people, particularly inner-city youth, to golf. It's a satisfying way to give something

back to the game. Here are programs you could team up with:

Hook a Kid on Golf (www.hookakid ongolf.com). Its mission is to encourage kids to play, by providing starter clubs, free lessons, and free greens fees.

The First Tee Program (thefirsttee .com), sponsored by the World Golf Foundation, offers affordable golf to those beginners, especially kids, who ordinarily would not have the opportunity to learn and play.

The Evans Scholars Foundation (evansscholarsfoundation.com), sponsored by the Western Golf Association, administers the largest privately funded college scholarship program in the United States to hundreds of deserving caddies each year.

The United States Golf Association Foundation (usga.com) promotes junior golf.

The Multicultural Golf Association of America (www.mgaa.com) believes that golf is for everyone. It sponsors a Junior Golf Program for inner-city and at-risk children. Its mission includes promoting

Members of Wake
Robin Golf Club

Courtesy Wake Robin Golf Club

education and positive values, free golf clinics, college scholarships, and possible careers in the golf industry.

Wake Robin Golf Club

Taking its name from the colorful spring wildflower, *Trillium erectum*, the Wake Robin Golf Club provides an inspiring account of claiming the right to golf. A group of African-American women whose husbands played golf met in 1936 to establish a golf club. Blacks had been associated with golf from before the Civil War when slaves caddied for their masters, but afterwards blacks were only allowed on courses as construction workers, food servers, and caddies. However, by playing on "caddies days" and after hours, black men did play, sometimes scoring in the low 70s.

The Wake Robin Club is credited for opening the doors of golf to black women. Members of Wake Robin had to overcome both racism and sexism, but they were determined. In 1938 they succeeded in getting Harold Ickes, then

Secretary of Interior, to approve construction of a golf course, now Langston Golf Course, and in 1941 to open all the District's public facilities including golf courses to minorities.

Members of Wake Robin had to endure poor playing conditions (Langston was built on a former dump), racist and sexist taunts, golf balls hit at them, stones thrown at them, and other harassment, but they prevailed. Wake Robin today is still a thriving club, proud of its long tradition and of such specific accomplishments as organizing tournaments for black professionals and helping to desegregate the PGA in 1961.

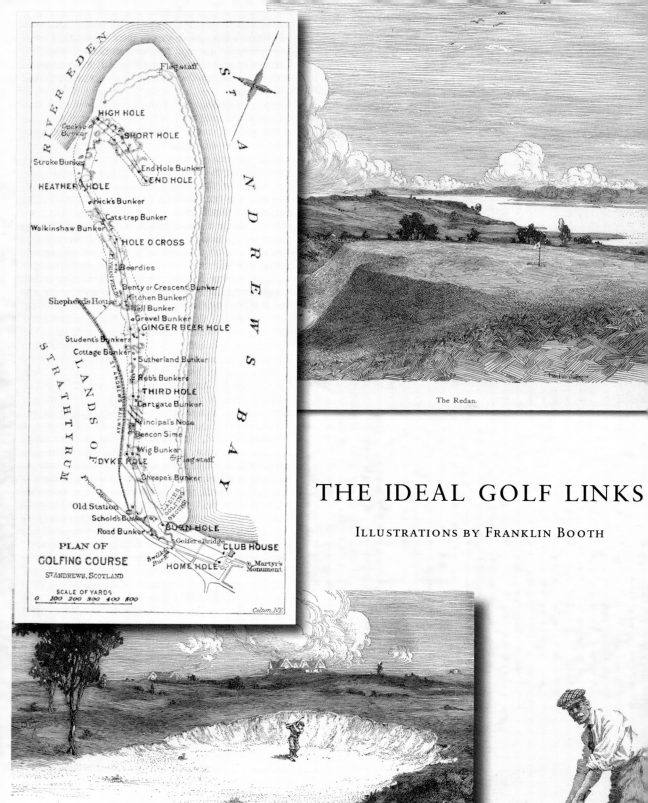

THE IDEAL GOLF LINKS

ILLUSTRATIONS BY FRANKLIN BOOTH

The Redan.

Home hole.

THE LAY
OF THE LAND

"I always attempt not only to make every hole different on a golf course, but never conspicuously to reproduce two exactly similar holes. I attempt to get inspiration by seizing on any natural features and accentuating the best golfing points on them."

—Alister MacKenzie,
Golf Architecture

Golf courses are the nonconformists of ball-playing sports. Tennis and basketball courts, soccer and football fields, baseball diamonds, bowling alleys, and pool tables, all adhere to uniform standards of length, width, surface texture, and shape. Not so golf courses. A golf course is a free-form expression of a course architect's imagination. Someone has developed a unique plan for every course. There, art and nature combine.

If you want to truly enjoy the game of golf, enjoy the extraordinary beauty and artistry of the courses where it is played. An understanding of the basic principles of course and hole design will help you here.

"In planning a golf course there are no fixed rules to which it is compulsory to conform, and the variety which results is one of the charms of the game."

—C.H. Alison, *The Golden Age of Golf Design*

The Old Course at St. Andrews, Scotland, is the model upon which all golf courses are patterned. It breathes the true spirit of golf course design conceived centuries ago by golfers who played the game over a links landscape, the area between beach and arable land that borders estuaries along the North Sea. It evolved over time as people with different skills and equipment played the game on a sand dune landscape. The course was simply laid out and changed by the players themselves to suit their needs.

Golf course architects? The winds.

Courtesy Robert Graves

Large sand bunker on Old St. Andrews course

Greens keepers? The sheep. Irrigation? The rain. All golf courses today owe their existence to the Scottish course. It is as if seeds from some great, archetypal Scottish national course have been carried by the winds and have sprouted all over the world.

THE DESIGNER'S PALETTE

Recreational golfers take pleasure from the site and the personality of each course. Part of the strong attraction of playing golf springs from the course itself, the sheer beauty of the vegetation, the topographic changes, and the wildlife. No wonder we experience a feeling of well-being, whether we play alone or in congenial company. Each course possesses its own magnetism, challenges, and special charm.

A course can be evaluated for its strategic and scoring challenges—distances, routes to a particular green, difficulty. But a recreational golfer can also focus on its sights, sounds, natural fragrances, and other sensory and aesthetic qualities. Holes flow towards and away from each other with a rhythm as we play. Tees, greens, fairways, roughs, and hazards are all connected and create distinctive scenic and dramatic effects.

Golf courses combine the wonders of nature with the special artistry of a

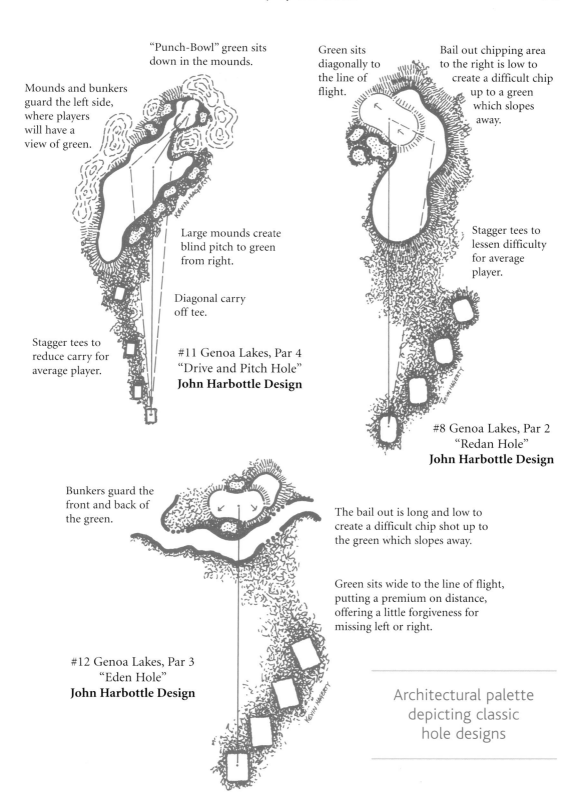

"Punch-Bowl" green sits down in the mounds.

Mounds and bunkers guard the left side, where players will have a view of green.

Large mounds create blind pitch to green from right.

Diagonal carry off tee.

Stagger tees to reduce carry for average player.

#11 Genoa Lakes, Par 4
"Drive and Pitch Hole"
John Harbottle Design

Green sits diagonally to the line of flight.

Bail out chipping area to the right is low to create a difficult chip up to a green which slopes away.

Stagger tees to lessen difficulty for average player.

#8 Genoa Lakes, Par 2
"Redan Hole"
John Harbottle Design

Bunkers guard the front and back of the green.

The bail out is long and low to create a difficult chip shot up to the green which slopes away.

Green sits wide to the line of flight, putting a premium on distance, offering a little forgiveness for missing left or right.

#12 Genoa Lakes, Par 3
"Eden Hole"
John Harbottle Design

Architectural palette
depicting classic
hole designs

Courtesy Dave Werschkul

natural beauty around us when we play. We move about in a surpassingly lovely landform, part garden, part park, and part playing field. To be conscious of the beauty around us heightens our enjoyment of the game. The trick is to be able to appreciate the choice and arrangement of each hole, the unified design, and the landscaped art form we play in.

> **Tip:** The next time you play, imagine the personalities of each of the individual holes. Are they secretive, shy, bold, boring, heroic, risky, mysterious, playful?

*Kona Country Club Golf Course,
Kona, Hawaii*

landscape architect. Water, trees and other vegetation, open space, rocks, hills, valleys, and slopes comprise the course designer's palette. The canvas is the land itself. Sky, horizon, scenic vistas, wind, and changes in light and shade contribute subtle shadings. For recreational players, the beauty of the course and the infinite variety of conditions constitute some of the chief delights of the sport.

It's hard not to be attracted to the

THE MAGIC OF A GREAT GOLF HOLE

Golf courses come in an inexhaustible variety of shapes and sizes. Thank goodness. Nothing could be more uninviting than 18 straight, 400-yard, "bowling alley" holes, arranged side by side and flanked by trees standing at silent attention.

The distance that the beginning, intermediate, or expert golfer typically hits shots influences the architect's design of individual holes. Some are savage doglegs with bunkers stoutly defending their greens. Others offer us hidden greens requiring divine guidance. Some have wide fairways leading to small greens; others, narrow fairways opening to tiered greens of vast acreage. A good architect blends challenge and relief for every level of player on each hole.

A course designer, much like the magician who practices the art of illusion, frequently uses topographic deception to create special effects and even a false sense of reality. Alister MacKenzie, trained in camouflage while serving in the British Army as a medical doctor during World War I, applied many of these principles when he began his career as a golf course architect. In his courses, the placement of bunkers and the shaping of the fairways disguised both distances and the

Alister Mackenzie, the great recreational golf course architect (1870-1934)

Courtesy Pasatiempo Golf Course

sizes of the greens. Undulating, open fairways, greens tucked away in the sand dunes, and ocean horizons created an illusion of difficulty or a false sense of ease. Certain holes have special effects that can trick a golfer into shot-making strategies which are challenging yet fun.

Mike and I enjoy shots which force us to carry over a canyon, pond, or lake. We have sent many golf balls to a watery resting place by misjudging shots that seem farther than they really are. Standing over a chasm or body of water usually intimidates me, and I will frequently over-compensate, swing too hard, and hit the ball into the area that I dread the most. Sometimes I think that dragons are real. They hang around those magical holes and eat my errant golf balls.

"The vital thing about a hole is that it should either be more difficult than it looks or more difficult than it is. It must never be as it looks."
—Walter Simpson

WHAT'S IN A NAME?

A course may be predominantly flat, rolling, or heavily treed. Each one has a unique personality that distinguishes it from all others. A course that is not designed around a particular shot pattern, such as a slice, will interest a greater number of players. Too much repetition is boring. A well-designed course allows players of all skill levels to demonstrate their abilities. The great courses and golf holes stand out from the rest because of their differences and not their adherence to some standard "cookie-cutter mold."

"Variety is the spice of golf, just as it is in life."

—Donald Ross, in *The Golden Age of Golf Design*

Bandon Dunes in Oregon is a classic links course that was built on a large sand dune formation overlooking the Pacific Ocean. Many holes highlight distinctive landscape features such as ridges, valleys, hills, capes, dells, sand dunes, flowering gorges, and streams.

Architects will often utilize natural features to accentuate or define a classic hole. For example, a "dell" can often turn out to be a hidden hole. A "knoll," often called "the Alps," can hide a green and create a blind shot. A "cape," or point of land, is frequently used by architects to set up a risk or reward shot that challenges the golfer to bring the ball toward the water in order to gain a shorter route to the green. A "valley" configuration will allow a ball to

bounce off the sides and roll onto the fairway. A "ridge" shape is the reverse of the valley and will require the golfer to keep the ball in the center of the fairway, or risk it falling off the ridge into the rough.

Some of the most interesting and challenging golf courses and holes are associated with natural features, historical places, or famous people. Wentworth golf course in Surrey, England, is affectionately known as "The Burma Road" because of its length.

Sometimes, individual or groups of

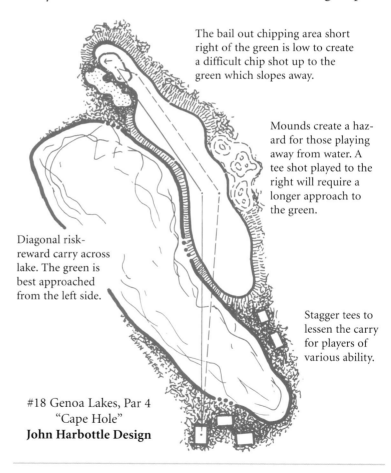

The bail out chipping area short right of the green is low to create a difficult chip shot up to the green which slopes away.

Mounds create a hazard for those playing away from water. A tee shot played to the right will require a longer approach to the green.

Diagonal risk-reward carry across lake. The green is best approached from the left side.

Stagger tees to lessen the carry for players of various ability.

#18 Genoa Lakes, Par 4
"Cape Hole"
John Harbottle Design

Cape hole design

"The Alps," an example of a classic ridge or hilltop hole

"The Sahara," an example of a large sand bunker on a Scottish links course

holes have names that indicate their particular character. "Amen Corner," the 11th, 12th, and 13th holes at Augusta, were christened by Herb Wind, the great American golf writer, who thought prayer helped get through them without disaster. "Mae West" refers to striking twin mounds that grace the 12th hole at the Bel-Air Country Club. The 15th hole at Winged Foot was called "The Pyramid" because its elevated green made golfers feel they were aiming for the apex of a pyramid. "Hell's Half Acre" refers to the 7th hole at Pine Valley and its vast sand waste guarding the approach to the green. These names suggest the measure of respect, even affection, golfers have felt for these holes.

"The site of a golf course should be there, not brought there."
—Perry Maxwell, in *The Golden Age of Golf Design*

PRINCIPLES OF COURSE DESIGN

Early Scottish courses hardly changed the landscape. They were laid out on links land along the undulating coastal sand dunes and depressions. Later they were followed by the "heath" courses built upon inland sandy soils. In general,

Steam driven mower and roller, c. 1906

Designed by nature

"There is nothing on this course that is made by man. Golfers play on it. But the architect of the land . . . is God."
—Caddy Dave Hutchinson of the Old Course at St. Andrews

early courses were constructed on existing topographic features with little alteration of the surroundings.

Subsequent course architects altered the natural landscape more severely. Some used earth-moving machinery, pumps, and other mechanized aids. They configured courses to accommodate mechanical mowers and rollers, being sure to provide enough fairway between green and rough for the mowers to pass. They planted both natural and introduced vegetation.

Today's courses are a blend of the Scottish "design by nature" and the later "designed by people" concepts. Some architects choose to "discover" the course in the existing topography; some "create" the course by modifying or shaping the land. Others do a little of both. The types of design philosophy—by nature, by people, blend—offer us distinctly different golfing experiences.

A designed-by-nature course is never completely unaltered, but it does retain many of the natural elements original to the terrain. You'll know this type of course when you see:

1) mostly unaltered landforms. Links courses use existing sand dune formations. Other golf landscapes use existing ravines, hills, and swales. Tees and greens are sited on naturally occurring plateaus.

2) vegetation that appears much like surrounding vegetation. It is native to the locale and does not seem out of place or introduced.

3) lakes, rivers, streams, wetlands, and the sea incorporated into the design theme to become part of the challenge and beauty of the course. Holes are placed with little alteration of the land.

When you play such courses, you feel you are moving in a place that is in absolute harmony with its surroundings. Spectacular effects can be achieved. Greens, poised on seaside headlands, command breathtaking views. The course design melds into the setting. If you like an uncontrived

A designed-by-nature course follows natural contours.

feel to your surroundings, you will like this brand of course.

Designed by people

"In golf construction art and utility meet; both are absolutely vital; one is utterly ruined without the other."
—George Thomas, in *Golf Architecture in America*

A designed-by-people course takes much of its character from manmade changes to the landscape and vegetation. You see this type of course in urban and other areas that lack natural features to incorporate into the course. Artificial elements can contribute

beauty and variety to an otherwise undistinguished environment. A gifted designer who has access to a good site, proper materials, and maintenance can recreate a classic "punch-bowl" hole that in links courses was designed to hold water and contain a shot.

You can spot the more imposed types of courses when you see the following:

1) raised greens in otherwise flat landscapes. Greens may mimic natural undulations and slopes.
2) artificial ponds, bio-swales, and wetlands that provide scenic relief and biological diversity.

A "punch-bowl hole," from a traditional Scottish links course

They enhance play and also help filter runoff water and provide homes for wildlife.

3) trees and other vegetation planted along tees, fairways, greens, and roughs. They create interesting hazards, provide shade and habitat, and contribute to overall course design.

On courses that combine golf with gardening and landscape architecture, you get an impression of walking through an 18th-century park. Spectacular flowering shrubs line a fairway, dense ferns guide golfers from the green to the next tee, and pale sand bunkers defend greens. The creative architect uses art and nature to achieve stunningly beautiful effects.

FROM TEE TO GREEN

"A round of golf should provide eighteen inspirations—not necessarily thrills, for spectacular holes may be sadly overdone. Every hole may be constructed to provide charm without being obtrusive about it."
—A.W. Tillinghast,
Golf Architecture

Each of the features of a golf course makes a particular contribution to the course designer's layout and to our pleasure in playing.

Tip: Take a camera with you. We know one golfer who does pen and ink sketches and watercolors in winter months based on summer photographs.

Courtesy Jason Moss

Golfer on tee box

Tee

A tee is usually elevated, if ever so slightly. From this vantage point, take a moment to survey the entire hole. Obviously, the tee is the place to plan your shot. You'll note the shape of the hole, distance to the green, location of sand bunkers, water features, and other hazards crucial to your decisions about what club to use and where the ball should land.

Tip: As you are about to tee off, pause and enjoy the scenery. This is one of 18 scenic vistas, the kinds of postcard views drivers pull off highways to appreciate.

Fairway

The wide band of groomed, mowed turf grass that connects tee to green is the best route to the green. Mike and I have tried other routings—rough and water—and we can attest that the fairway, the "short grass," is the best place to be. The fairway joins tee, green, and hazards to unify the golf hole.

The fairway usually contains one or more optimum landing zones for the next shot. Its shape can vary from straight to dogleg right or left. Though it is rare, my favorite hole is one where you can't see the green from the fairway. The fairway can also be a social area where there is time while walking or riding in a cart to talk with other golfers.

"The principal consideration of the architect is to design his course in such a way as to hold the interest of the player from the first tee to the last green and to present the problems of the various holes in such a way that they register in the player's mind as he stands on the tee or on the fairway for the shot to the green."

—William Flynn, in *The Golden Age of Golf Design*

Tip: When a fairway is absent and you must, for example, hit from tee to green over water or an unplayable hazard, the architect is challenging you both technically and psychologically: How good is your aim? How steady your nerves? Savor the challenge.

The world is all before them.

Hazards

Without these "trouble-ahead" areas, golf would not be half as much fun. Hazards lend special interest to many a hole. Placements of sand and grassy bunkers, water features, tall and short roughs, gullies, ditches, and out-of-bounds areas help create the character of a hole and the particular challenges we face. Far from being the

Courtesy Bandon Dunes Golf Course, Bandon, OR

Bandon Dunes pot bunker hazard

Courtesy Robert Glusic, wildernessvideo.com

Enjoying golf in tall rough

dreaded monsters of a course, for the recreational golfer, hazards covey excitement, or challenge, or frustration, but never boredom.

Hazards punish the golfer who cannot hit straight or who hits too long or too short. The most severe hazards often require a "carry" over the danger zone. One of the most feared is open water, and many a golfer, when facing a simple carry of 100 yards, will top a ball, sending it to a watery grave.

"O! cursed be the hand that made these fatal holes,
Cursed the heart that had the heart to do it!"
　　　　　—Shakespeare, *King Richard III*

These hazards cause hesitation and confusion, or worse, doubt. What iron to hit? What direction to take? They introduce another level of complexity and challenge, prompting us to think carefully and look both ways before we hit.

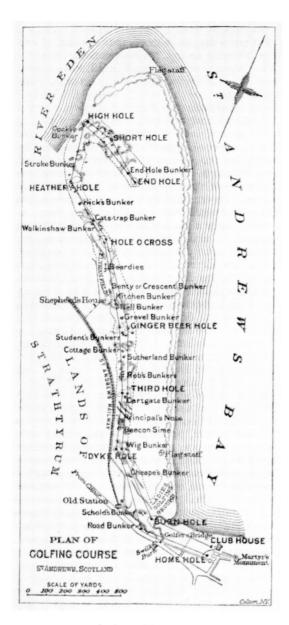

*Course map of The Old Course, St. Andrews,
showing the famous hazards and holes*

Some hazards are strategically placed to require a choice between a risky but more advantageous long shot and a surer but less desirable safe shot. Elements of risk and reward play a big

part in the design of many holes, and better courses offer relatively more opportunities for such decisions for players of all abilities.

"A narrow plateau for a green, or a few hummocks in front of one, will very likely cause just as much trouble and amusement to a player as a gaping chasm stretching right across the course."
                    —Harry S. Colt,
                    Golf Architecture

On many courses, especially older ones, hazards have been named after some defining incident, some memorable character who haunted the course, or simply the look of the hazard. Each of the more than 100 bunkers at St. Andrews Old Course are named. Some of the more famous include "The Principal's Nose," "Wig Bunkers," "The Beardies," "The Crescent," "The Kitchen," "The Scholars," and "The Hell Bunker." Another bunker on the same course, higher than "The Hell Bunker," is called "The Pulpit" because Hell can be seen from it. It is difficult to say, until you are in one of these bunkers, whether the nickname subliminally increases or diminishes the fearfulness of your lie.

Green

Ah, the green. The golf hole terminates on the green, the stage for our grand finale where we reassemble, strut our various roles, and watch each other putt. Here our energy and attention shift from power to precision, finesse, and fine motor skills. Here we must "read the green" to interpret the probable path our ball will take to the cup through the undulations that course architects have left behind to challenge us.

> **Tip:** Red, white, and blue flags on the pin are often used to indicate pin placement relative to the near, middle, or back side of the green respectively. Or pennants can be placed low, in the middle, or high on the pin to denote close, mid, or far cup placement.

Greens vary considerably from small, flat, round surfaces to large, complex, multi-tiered shapes. Generally, larger greens are built to accommodate lots of foot traffic during a long golf season. Greens can be sculpted out of flat lands or sited on raised platform areas.

"Putting greens are to a golf courses what faces are to portraits."
—Charles Blair Macdonald,
Scotland's Gift—Golf

The approach to a green is a crucial element in overall hole design. Course architects aim at balancing the size of the hazard-free area around the hole with the difficulty level of the approach. Bunkers around greens add drama and require us to pause and plan our shots. Some greens leave an open approach area so the ball can easily bounce and roll on. Others, especially par-3 holes, can be surrounded by bunkers and require the first shot to land on the green, on the fly, with no run-up. Well-watered greens can hold an aerial shot, but hard greens require a run-up.

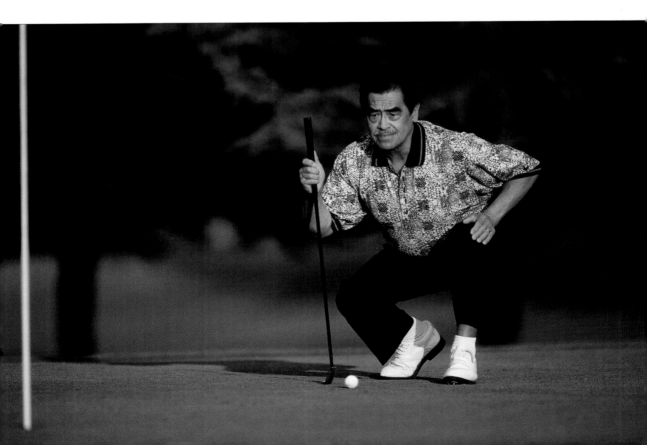

Tip: If you play spring or fall golf, expect "frost delays" during cold weather. Footprints can severely damage frost-covered greens. Your start will be delayed until the frost melts.

Putting surfaces vary. Some greens are uniformly flat or tilted; others may have subtle undulations that move a ball in several different directions en route to the pin. Green speed varies with the slope. Fast greens generally average up to a 5% slope, with slower greens up to about a 1% slope.

HOW TO FIND YOUR WAY

It can be a bit daunting to find your way around an unfamiliar course. The easiest solution is to play with someone who knows the course. Then you will know where to pay for the round, find the first tee, get around the course, and you will get acquainted with local conventions and etiquette. But if that isn't possible, you can use your scorecard or yardage booklet as a navigation tool.

"A mighty maze but not without a plan."
        —Alexander Pope,
          Essay on Man

Your scorecard is your map

Most golfers know that to find your way around an unfamiliar course you use the diagram on the back of the scorecard. It depicts the course layout, the shape of individual holes, locations and types of hazards, and distances from tee to green. The scorecard also gives you the relative difficulty of each hole in numbers from 1 to 18, 1 being the most difficult hole on the course. That way, you know on which holes you get or give strokes when you are playing competitive golf. For instance, if you are playing match play and your handicap entitles you to four strokes from your opponent, you deduct one stroke from your score on each of the four most difficult holes. If you are playing stroke play, you simply deduct four strokes from your total score.

As you play, you can compare the difficulty rating with your impressions of the hole design, the types and frequency of hazards, shape of the fairway, ball landing zones, and topographic complexity. Note whether there is an elevated tee or elevated green. Examining the difficulty rating of each hole before you play it will alert you to special features. Difficulty ratings will also give you an index of how strategically you must play. A difficult hole may require a long iron or accurate placement of shots for you to be successful.

Your yardage booklet, your other map

Many courses have a "yardage booklet" available. This is a short booklet that provides detailed information on hole layout, distances from the tee to hazards and from the tee to the green. Size and slope of the green are indicated. The scorecard and the yardage booklet will provide you with an in-depth understanding to improve your shot planning and enjoyment of the holes.

SOMETHING FOR EVERYONE

A round of golf should inspire, challenge, and excite players of all abilities. A good architect designs a course that is difficult enough to hold the interest of the truly competitive golfer and still be playable and captivating for the recreational golfer.

Some owners and architects build with the eye of an artist. They want to create something special out of the natural landscape, a course that will inspire golfers for centuries. Others build courses to incorporate golf with a housing development. If, after you have played a course a few times, it does not feel right, choose another.

Alister MacKenzie, the great Scottish course architect of the 1920s and 1930s, was one of the first to recognize the importance of building courses suitable

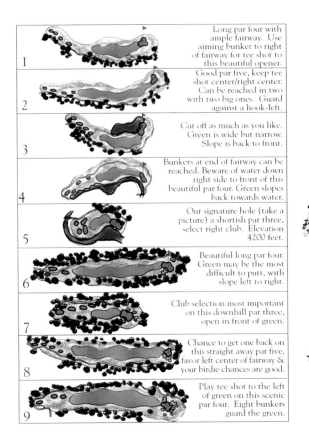

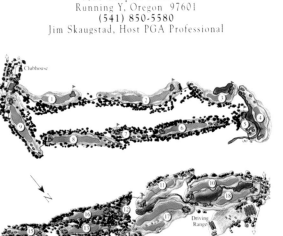

Scorecard from Running Y Golf Course, Running Y, Oregon

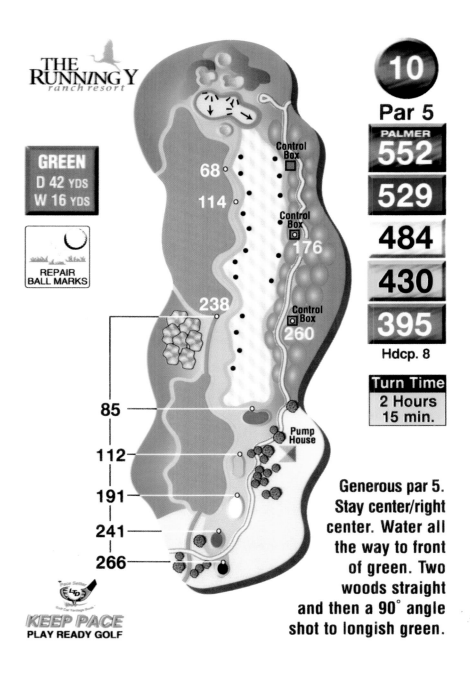

THE
RUNNING Y
ranch resort

GREEN
D 42 YDS
W 16 YDS

REPAIR
BALL MARKS

68
114
238

Control
Box
176

Control
Box
260

Control
Box

Pump
House

85
112
191
241
266

10
Par 5

PALMER
552
529
484
430
395
Hdcp. 8

Turn Time
2 Hours
15 min.

Generous par 5.
Stay center/right
center. Water all
the way to front
of green. Two
woods straight
and then a 90° angle
shot to longish green.

KEEP PACE
PLAY READY GOLF

Courtesy Running Y Ranch Resort,
Klamath Falls, OR

Page from yardage booklet

for the average golfer. MacKenzie tried hard to develop alternative routes to the holes for golfers of all abilities. He built both to challenge and inspire. His holes are fun to play.

> **Tips:** To better appreciate a course, ask the following questions at the pro shop:
>
> 1) Which are the most scenic holes?
> 2) Are there any special plants (a 300-year-old oak) or animals (elk, deer, foxes) to watch for?
> 3) When was the course built? What was here before the golf course? Any local history?

". . . you rarely hear of anyone taking their score at Alwoodley; they get quite enough fun in trying to beat their doughty opponents and trying to conquer the varied and difficult holes of the course."

—Alister MacKenzie, *The Spirit of St. Andrews*

Tom Doak, a contemporary course architect, feels his responsibility is to heighten the challenge of play without discouraging players. As he puts it in his book, *Anatomy of a Golf Course,* "The golf course is only a medium which makes the game more interesting; it is not supposed to be an obstacle course, eliminating the player who trips up first." A

good course makes us feel good about the game, our playing companions, the golfing experience, and ourselves. When a course is exciting, we can enjoy ourselves even if we are not scoring well.

Course Appreciation 101

Don't let yourself trudge around a course, concentrating only on your line of sight between your ball and the next hole. Pause to enjoy the beauty of the course and of individual holes. Notice how fairways and grassy mounds are set in the surrounding landscape. There may be symmetry or asymmetry in the placement of bunkers down a fairway and around a green. There are rhythms in the alternations of holes—

Courtesy Robert Glusic wildernessvideo.com

The eighth hole at Stone Ridge Golf Course, Medford, Oregon

hard or easy, long or short, flat or contoured. Trees, flowers, bushes, undulating grasses, rock outcroppings, and sparkling water can induce anxiety or peaceful harmony.

Being alert to design concepts as we play helps us see the dynamics of the course and leads us to a higher level of appreciation. As you play, observe:

1) Do the bunkers "fit" their greens? How are they arranged? Is their size right?

2) Is there a pattern in the arrangement of bunkers and trees? On our home course, there are sycamore "marker trees" planted 150 yards from each hole.

3) Is there a rhythm as you move from hole to hole? Do holes with wide fairways and forgiving roughs give you some breathing room for more challenging holes with narrow fairways?

4) Is there a harmonious linkage of tee, fairway, rough, and green?

5) Are the par 3s, 4s, and 5s arranged in a sequence that is interesting?

Signature holes

Another way to enjoy a course is to be alert for the so-called "signature hole," the hole that acts as the architect's signature on the canvas of the

Courtesy Dave Werschkul

The famous seventh hole at Pebble Beach Golf Course, Pebble Beach, California

land. This hole possesses distinctive features that set it apart from all others. It has a unique personality. A stunning view from the top of the 9th or 18th tee leading into the clubhouse may be the one. Or it may be a hole that plays over a river or next to a waterfall. Some "signature" holes are too gimmicky and showy, such as an artificial island in a lake. These holes may be poorly designed and seem out of place.

RATING COURSES

The next time you play, give the course a "playability and unique design test." As you play, evaluate the holes and the entire course for architectural beauty and enjoyment. All you need is a score card to mark each hole with the appropriate number of stars. Look for obvious features that seem either harmonious or out of place.

"As with great classical movements, they are complete with exhilaration and excitement, a blend of all that's good and gone before in the music or golf design. The very best final holes are played with the setting sun behind to afford players and spectators alike all the splendor of the landscape's shadows coupled with the finest review of shots played in full portrait aesthetics."

—Jimmy Kidd, golf course architect

For example, stand on the tee or some elevated spot and look at the shapes, colors, and textures of the fairways, greens, roughs, and hazards. Get a feel for an individual hole by taking a few moments to look before you hit your tee shot. As you move towards the green, let your senses guide your evaluation. Mike and I have played on courses that landed in the one star category because of an uninteresting, featureless layout, boring fairways, flat "postage-stamp" greens, no water or other challenging hazards.

On the other hand, we've played several courses running along sand bluffs above Pacific Ocean waves and another that skirts a wild, cascading river. We've played at the base of a jagged, snow-capped mountain and flirted with the fringes of a desert arroyo as it descended through a forest of giant Cardon cacti before joining the Sea of Cortez. At River Falls, Wisconsin, the third, fourth, and fifth holes drop steeply downhill until you're so far below the level of the rest of the course that you have to hop a funicular back to the top.

Some courses may rate less than four stars, but they may still have a few sensational holes that make the course worth playing. One has a waterfall along the edge of a raised emerald green, and the music of the water fills the air. On another course, two jealous male turkeys guarding their female harem accosted my playing partner and me. They succeeded in driving us off the fairway! The hole was not memorable, but the possibility of being challenged by turkeys in full-feathered array keeps us going back.

Wild turkeys add color and excitement to the game.

The psychology of a course, the mental tension it induces, and your overall course strategy are also important considerations for judging. Does the course provide more than one approach to the green or several ways to play the hole? Do you challenge yourself with a big "risk-reward" shot that may carry you over the pond to the green in two shots, or do you take the safe route around the pond and hit the green in three shots? Can the course offer you a new challenge every time you play, or is it boring after the first time? Do natural features such as water, trees, canyons, wild flowers, or topography draw you back? The best course designs balance illusion and deception to create memorable and enjoyable golf experiences for golfers of all abilities.

When compiling your rating, decide whether the unique features of a hole and a course add to your overall enjoyment. A three can be given to a memorable hole, a four, to a hole that you would want to play again and again. You might want to keep the rating cards, plus any notes you care to make on them, long after the scorecards have been thrown away.

The "Enjoyment Rating" for each hole

When the course is not crowded and you have a little more time, keep an "enjoyment score" of each hole. Here is a simple rating system:

★ = ho hum, boring
★★ = interesting, I'd like to play that again
★★★ = very good, lots to see and appreciate there
★★★★ = a memorable hole, a personal favorite

"Upon the manner in which the fairway is set—at any rate, at the longer holes—depends the greater part of the interest of the hole. If it appears plain and obvious, it is insipid and lacks character; but, laid out with ingenuity and imagination, it can please by the grace of its setting and intrigue the golfer by the particular problem that he has to solve to the best of his ability."
    —H.N. Wethered and Tom Simpson, *The Architectural Side of Golf*

Forget your own score when you rate holes. Ask yourself only whether they are inspiring to play. Here are additional criteria for rating a hole:

1) variety of views
2) sheer beauty of the hole
3) golfing challenge (difficult carry, narrow fairway, well-bunkered green)
4) diversity of play (doglegs right or left, raised greens, blind shots)

5) harmony of hole, a sense of balance
6) rhythm of play, nice alternation in difficulty, length
7) ambient noise: pleasant, natural sounds or disturbing traffic noises
8) wildlife seen
9) plays well in all weather

The ranking of each hole can then be totaled for a course ranking with which you can compare golfing experiences.

"The course of true golf never did run smooth."
    —Henny Youngman

" *She bleated : ' G-o-o-d, g-o-o-o-d, ind-e-e-e-d ! ' "*

GOLFING WITH
GREEN GLASSES

The purple light leans
long shadows over greens.
Evening loon calls still.

Haiku golfing poets, golf course architects, and regular players alike can be charmed by the untamed natural beauty that wildlife brings to each golf course. Why not combine the pleasure of being outdoors golfing with an opportunity to appreciate the wildlife that inevitably presents itself?

COMBINING GOLF WITH A NATURE WALK

Sensitivity to natural surroundings can enhance the quality of the game for a recreational golfer who is able to see a

A birdwatcher's scorecard from an Audubon certified course

A red-tail hawk swoops in for the kill on the ninth hole.

connection between the course and the natural world. Mike and I believe that environmental awareness increases our enjoyment of the game. Natural history is our silent playing partner.

Birds and birdies

Bird watching and golf are both very popular (actually birdwatchers outnumber golfers two to one). Both involve walking outdoors in a setting filled with living things. Many bird watchers keep score by compiling a "life list" of all the species that they identify. Some golf courses have scorecards, which indicate the types of birds that can be seen on the course.

I personally enjoy the birding opportunities that present themselves while I play. Watching a hawk circling in a thermal current or a tree full of cedar waxwings feeding on berries always adds value to my golf game, especially the time we saw a large red-tailed hawk take a coot.

"My favorite activity while golfing on my local course is to watch a particular family of Canadian geese raise their goslings."
—Alan W., retired university registrar

Carry a pair of binoculars and a bird book with you to help you identify birds that you will see on the golf course.

The extra magnification can also be useful for locating landing areas, hazards, and the general lay of the land. Always be sure that you do not hold up play by taking too much time for your enjoyment of nature. Early mornings as well as the hour before dusk are the best times for viewing wildlife as well as enjoying sunrises or sunsets. These times can be spectacular for taking photographs, so consider packing a camera in your bag.

Waterfowl migrations in the fall or spring are magnificent to behold, but, depending on your location, you might also see alligators basking in the short grass next to the pond. Or, if you're lucky, you could see bald eagles perched in the spruce snag in the river and others feeding on spawning salmon. Did you notice the cougar tracks in the sand trap next to the lake? How about that herd of elk in the distance?

Smell the flowers

Nature's beauty is in the mind of the beholder. Some golfers only see that their ball landed in the rough. "Green golfers," however, take note of the native grasses, oak woodland, pine forest, or poison oak patch that just ate their drive. Bright azaleas, wild dogwood, striking camas lilies, bachelor buttons, and other wildflowers wait patiently for us. All we have to do is attentively look

their way. Springtime flowers and fall colors beckon me to play golf, just to see the seasonal changes reflected in the vegetation.

> **TIP:** Notice what kind of food is available to wildlife (e.g., berries, seeds, nuts, fruit, grass, small prey, etc.).

As you walk to your ball, look at the variety of flowers and the color of the birds, hear the many sounds coming from the pond or woods, smell the sweet fragrance of the trees. As you assess the lie of your ball, note the surroundings—the flatness or tilt of the land. Watch the butterfly as it lands on your ball.

Wildlife friendly courses

Do you see boxes along the wooded edges of fairways or roughs? Bird boxes and bat boxes are sometimes

A kaleidoscope of wildflower color in a butterfly garden

Courtesy Quail Ridge Golf and Country Club, Boynton Beach, FL

Chamomile flowers. One person's rough is another person's cup of tea.

strips) designed to treat runoff from greens, tees, and equipment-washing areas. Many courses have constructed valuable artificial water features such as ponds, streams, and wetlands. By playing them regularly, we can encourage the "wildlife friendly" courses that practice good wildlife stewardship.

A WALK ON THE WILD SIDE

Carrying your golf clubs around a course in pursuit of your occasionally elusive ball can be frustrating. Sometimes taking a wildlife break can introduce a calming, even humorous influence. Who knows? A bird seen on the course may encourage a birdie on the next hole. A number of golfers have described an enjoyable moment watching a family of geese or a circling turkey vulture or a herd of deer. Observing a flock of mallard ducks feeding with only the "butts up" portions of their tail feathers showing can be enjoyable. And

erected to attract birds and bats to golf courses as a means of natural insect control in lieu of insecticides and other chemical management tools.

Some courses have vegetated wetlands, swales, and biofilters (grassy

Summer game . . . winter game at the V.A. Domiciliary, White City, Oregon

Restored wetland improves water quality and habitat.

if you play winter golf, how about those ducks ice skating on the pond next to the fairway?

The too blue heron
lines up a yellow perch
as a cloud passes the sun.

Many courses are a sanctuary for wildlife and provide for us an island of urban tranquility within a sea of congested humanity and turmoil. Birds, deer, and other wildlife love to feast on the abundant grass and prey. If we are alert to the wildlife and other natural attractions found on a course, we add considerable delight to our game.

TIP: Ask about what wildlife people have seen on your favorite courses. The presence of native waterfowl, wading birds, songbirds, hawks, deer, muskrats, beaver, native turtles, and others are all positive indicators of a healthy golf course.

O, GIVE ME A HOME

A golf course is a mosaic of different habitat types that blend the plant and animal communities into a playing field for our enjoyment. Mixed into the fairways, roughs, out of bounds, and greens is an ecosystem that supports

Courtesy Quail Ridge Golf and Country Club, Boynton Beach, FL

Critical habitat for endangered wood storks at Quail Ridge,
an award-winning Audubon Certified sanctuary

both natural and introduced plants and animal life.

Golf courses have distinct territories—perhaps of coyotes, deer, bobcats, turkeys, geese, hawks, and other animals—depending on subtle differences in vegetation, water, and topography. Sometimes the territory lines are invisible, marked only by scent, while other boundaries are more obvious if you pay a little attention. Mating territories, feeding lanes, and thick grass and brush cover are present on most golf courses.

As you walk the course and play your game, imagine the rough and other hazards as something far more significant to the life around you than the place where you just lost your best ball.

Golfing on the edge

The margins of puzzles are the key to understanding how the pieces go together. So are the edges of the rough, water hazards, out of bounds, greens, low bushes, high trees, and other defining lines and edges. These areas are the highways, motels, and fast food restaurants of the wildlife kingdom.

Have you ever noticed hawks perched on a fence, a grove of trees, or the side of a road? These birds of prey are watching for their rodent lunch that frequently travels the edges of the woodland foraging for food. The banks of ponds and streams create the rich niche of land and water that supports many creatures. Much like the watering holes in Kenya, the "casual water" found on courses is full of wildlife. You won't see a lion or a wildebeest, but you may spot a great blue heron, a box turtle, or perhaps even a cougar or fox taking a drink.

We golfers understand the concept of edges because playing the game involves knowing the best place to hit the ball for any given hole. Locating out of bounds or hazards is good course management. The next time you plan your shot from the tee, notice the wildlife habitat edges. As you are looking for your ball, imagine what creatures live in this area when golfers do not occupy it. If you train yourself, you will grow more alert to your local wild animals.

Course refuges

Some courses have been carefully developed to maintain biological diversity of flora and fauna by saving and planting native vegetation and creating places for both golfers and wildlife.

Courtesy Robert Glusic, wildernessvideo.com

Hazards for golfers, food and drink for wildlife, Myrtle Creek Golf Course, Myrtle Creek, Oregon

*Environmentally friendly tees
biodegrade quickly.*

Riparian vegetation along streams offers migration corridors and a sanctuary for wildlife as well as excellent lateral hazards.

In many areas, golf courses blend in well with existing wildlife habitats and provide subsidiary ecological niches, especially when water and wetlands are integrated into the landscape. Tall rough and buffer areas around the woodlands, ponds, and streams provide excellent wildlife habitat. These natural areas also lower the maintenance costs for these areas when compared to other sites requiring mowing, fertilizer, and irrigation.

"The creator of golf holes must not only possess imagination, but a keen appreciation of the offerings of nature, and the art of landscaping must be allied closely with that of the architect."
— A.W. Tillinghast, *Golf Architecture*

In some cases, a golf course protects the habitat for endangered species. For example, golfers in southern Florida can see endangered wood storks or alligators in the protected wetlands adjacent to the fairway. Some Washington State golfers enjoy watching salmon spawn in streams that run through their golf courses. Golfers in Kodiac, Alaska, have a truly exciting round of golf when they detour around a Kodiak bear feeding on salmon near the 18th green.

A greens keeper at a nearby golf course alerted us to the mountain lion tracks he frequently sees in some of the sand bunkers. Now, we check the bunkers for tracks before we hit our shots. Once when Mike and I were playing a links course on the coast, I noticed a bald eagle perched on a Sitka spruce tree next to the 17th hole. The eagle was taking advantage of the edge between the out-of-bounds canyon and the green and searching for rabbits or other prey. I feel, like Native

Courtesy Quail Ridge Golf and Country Club, Boynton Beach, FL

A wood duck box attracts visitors.

Americans before me, that an eagle is a good omen, and, sure enough, I sank my putt for a birdie.

> **TIP:** Follow the lead of birders, who keep life lists of species observed. Keep your own list of wildlife you see on the courses you play. It may be a better indicator of your enjoyment and satisfaction than your scorecard.

BEING KIND TO OUR WEB-FOOTED FRIENDS

While many of us golfers enjoy the wildlife experiences available on golf courses, motivated golfers can do more than just observe wildlife. Here are some ways to become pro-active in helping your golf course encourage, restore, and protect wildlife and its habitat:

1) Talk to the course pro or course manager about conducting an inventory of wildlife on your course. Suggest an Audubon Christmas bird count or other seasonal inventories.
2) Map the habitat and suggest ways of protecting the wildlife environment.
3) Ask the greens superintendent whether Best Management Practices and Integrated Pest Management Programs are being used on your course. These programs reduce the use of fertilizers and pesticides and promote wildlife habitat.

4) Promote wildlife education. Attractive interpretive signs describing the special features of a course can be placed all along the course. Natural history features can be explained by means of simple interpretive stations. High school or middle school teachers might welcome the opportunity as a hands-on-project for their classes.

5) Inquire about conservation easements and cooperative development strategies.

6) Ask about starting a volunteer "bird house program" on your course. Wood duck boxes, swallow boxes, bat houses, barn owl habitat, and goose nest platforms provide viewing opportunities and biological control of insects and rodents.

Courtesy Quail Ridge Golf and Country Club, Boynton Beach, FL

Environmental regulation

Wildlife protection, chemical management, water conservation, bioswales, water quality and wetlands—so what? Well, these issues contribute to the health of the environment and to public health, and they enhance the quality of play for golfers. Environmental regulations, which will be even stronger in the future, oversee the design and maintenance of golf courses. Now course developers and architects must take a proactive environmental position. The wisest golf course development and maintenance programs embrace a program of environmental advocacy and set examples for other courses.

A natural environment was the birthplace of golf, and that benchmark principle still guides designers and builders to use the principle of "design with nature" in their work. Water quality, water conservation, chemical management, and wildlife habitat improvement projects are being incorporated into the fabric of golf course construction and management. Golf courses can be both a home for wildlife and a playground for golfers. In fact, we think since wildlife was there first, it's the responsibility of course developers to maintain a natural habitat.

Audubon Cooperative Sanctuary Program

The Audubon Cooperative Sanctuary Program (ACSP) for golf courses "promotes ecologically sound land management and the conservation of our natural resources." (This program is not affiliated with the National Audubon Society.) The program includes six certification categories: Environmental Planning; Wildlife and Habitat Management; Integrated Pest Management; Water Conservation; Water Quality Management; and Outreach Education. This program also provides an advisory information service on how to conduct proactive environmental projects for golf courses. Currently there are over 2200 certified sanctuary programs in the United States, and the number is growing.

Flags flapping stiffly.
Songbirds seek leafy refuge.
Please, no rain for five more holes.

HEALING THE LAND

We are entering a renaissance golf age in which the very best minds and talents from many fields will come together to transform landscapes that have been neglected and abused into golf courses. Lands that were once toxic waste dumps or depleted agricultural fields or abandoned industrial sites are being restored and enhanced. Polluted waste water from these and other sites is being filtered and purified and returned to the streams to once again sustain native runs of trout and salmon. Flocks of migrating waterfowl and herds of deer and antelope are rediscovering these restored lands.

The following case studies describe courses that arose out of various environmental disasters.

Courtesy Quail Ridge Golf and Country Club, Boynton Beach, FL

Old Works Golf Course, Anaconda, Montana

A century old, 225-acre Anaconda copper mining site in Montana was declared a Superfund cleanup site due to the high volume of heavy metal shavings and arsenic by-products. The site was shut down in 1980, leaving the town of 10,000 with few economic options and many potentially harmful environmental consequences. The owners and community members decided to restore the site by building a golf course, something that had never been done before on a Superfund site.

The transformation of this toxic wasteland was a monumental task which required moving 1.3 million cubic yards of material, capping the site with limestone, adding 16 inches of clay, and finishing the top layer with eight inches of soil. Miles of drainage pipes and layers of PVC liners were

Courtesy Old Works Golf Course, Anaconda, MT

Before and after Superfund cleanup site

added to ensure that surface runoff did not penetrate into the ground water or flow into nearby Warm Springs Creek.

The end result is a Jack Nicklaus championship 7500-yard golf course that won second place for the most affordable new public course. In addition, the course won the 1999 Environmental Steward Award for National Public Courses.

The transformation of the contaminated Superfund site into the spectacular Old Works Golf Course has brought deer, elk, antelope, marmots, birds, and other wildlife back to this beautiful Montana valley. This site restoration has set a standard of environmental stewardship that is attracting worldwide attention.

The Quarry Golf Club, San Antonio, Texas

The Quarry Golf Club is a municipal public course situated on ground that comprised a portion of the Alamo Cement Company, which operated a limestone quarry there from 1920 until 1981. Planners faced significant problems on the 170-acre site, including the illegal dumping and stockpiling of 500,000 cubic yards of kiln dust. In addition, the lake at the bottom of the quarry was tied into San Antonio's water supply, which was in danger of being contaminated.

Engineers constructed clay-lined vaults to contain the kiln dust, and native soil was spread on top of the vaults and contoured and shaped into a beautiful 18-hole golf course. They

Before restoration

planted the course with a variety of native grasses, which have attracted many species of birds, mammals, and other wildlife. They routed the course along the lake, and a complex drainage system was installed to carry runoff water away from the lake where it is filtered through vegetative strips and bioswales and then returned back to the lake. A rigorous water quality-monitoring program is in place to insure that the filtering system is working correctly.

Many species of native and migratory songbirds, wading birds, birds of prey, and waterfowl now call The Quarry Golf Club home. The course works closely with the Audubon Cooperative Sanctuary Program and regulatory agencies to enhance and protect the habitat on the quarry site and its surrounding environment. The Quarry demonstrates how degraded land, once considered an eyesore and potential health hazard, can be reclaimed as a recreational amenity, a flourishing wildlife sanctuary, and a community asset.

Lazy Creek Restoration in the Rogue Valley, Oregon

Lazy Creek winds through the Rogue Valley Golf and Country Club (RVGCC) and provides the linkage for

Courtesy The Quarry Golf Club, San Antonio, TX

After restoration

During restoration

many of the holes in this traditional parkland course. I designed and supervised a large portion of the restoration of the creek recently in order to provide better water quality and wildlife habitat along with enhanced scenic appearance.

We removed exotic vegetation in the flood-plain zone and planted it with native sedges and rushes to restore the creek side and the wildlife corridor. We also added native willows and alders to stabilize the stream bank and to filter the urban runoff water. Several reaches of the creek were modified with stone walls to provide better flood protection and add an attractive visual quality to the Lazy Creek corridor. This project was a cooperative effort among the Oregon Division of State Lands, Mahar Homes Island Point Development, and the RVGCC.

NOT JUST FOR GOLFERS

The early Scottish links courses entertained many non-golfers: women drying clothes, soldiers drilling, fishermen mending their nets, children

Restored Lazy Creek, Rogue Valley Country Club, Medford, Oregon

Courtesy Robert Glusic, wildernessvideo.com

An urban oasis, Family Golf Center, Chicago, Illinois

playing, and forecaddies leading the way for their clients. There is no reason that golf courses can't serve multiple functions today.

Open space

Besides being a recreational area for a large golfing public, golf courses contribute to communities. They act as greenbelts and open space, allowing cities and suburbs to breathe. Large expanses of turf, trees, and other vegetation also provide temperature modification, noise abatement, erosion control, wind reduction, fresh air, and wildlife habitat. In addition, courses serve as a buffer for sensitive environmental areas, and some provide space for additional uses, such as cross-country track races, cross-country skiing, walking, and nature studies. Not least, golf courses reinforce the psychological and physical well being of people by providing a nearby, aesthetically pleasing natural setting.

Public access

Although in the past golf may have favored the exclusive use by a few at the expense of many, the race- and class-based stigmas associated with golf are rapidly disappearing. Today, golfers include people of all ages, genders, races, and economic means. Still, the cost can limit access to the sport.

How golf will continue to serve the needs of golfers and non-golfers alike is an open question. The future of course development is all over the map. At the high end, we see expensive courses developed in remote areas, offering expensive trips to rare and wonderful places—exotic getaway golf. Affordable golf becomes more difficult as construction and land costs rise. There is hope, however, because many municipal courses remain affordable, and inexpensive executive courses are becoming more popular for family golf outings.

But how can golf serve the non-golfing community? If new courses are going to be constructed or existing courses renovated, especially with public funds in urban areas, then the case must be made for public access to golf courses and multiple uses for them.

Community access is an important part of golf because it addresses the question of how to make the sport more available to a wider number of people. The following are some examples of ways courses can become part of the larger community:

1) Local courses can sponsor community outreach programs that offer a variety of introductory golf lesson packages, including reduced rates on lessons, equipment, and green fees.

2) Golf course tours for the public can acquaint potential new golfers with the course and the basic structure of the sport. Natural history tours can educate the general public to the value of courses for wildlife.

3) Some courses have public access trails around the edges of the course that are used for walking, jogging, cross-country training, botanizing, and other activities.

FUTURE GOLF

Future golf may also be played in wild and remote places accessible only by helicopter, boat, horseback, or rough backroads. This is true "getaway" golf. It's expensive, exotic, and it represents golf as it used to be played on the links courses of early Scotland. The courses are minimalist in design and are truly products of their natural landscapes. Old Tom Morris and Alister MacKenzie would be happy to play on these types of Scottish replicas.

"It's tough to make predictions, especially about the future."
—Yogi Berra

By the year 2050 it is estimated that there will be double the number of golfers today. Time constraints, land availability, multiple uses, course renovation, economics, new technology, and environmental concerns will define the golf courses of the future. Environmental constraints will place more restrictions on the use of water and chemicals, which in turn will affect the types of grasses and course designs.

Future courses may be browner than the emerald green oases that golfers are used to, but the technology for utilizing less water, fertilizer, pesticides, and fossil fuels may still allow many of them to retain that old-fashioned green look. Many courses will be built on reclaimed land that was once unusable. These sites, formerly considered health hazards, will be beautiful golf courses that support wildlife and contribute to the economic well-being of surrounding communities.

Many of the "older" courses will be restored to the architectural style of their period. New technologies for water conservation and use of chemicals will allow these courses to continue as examples of the "golden age of golf."

Imagine holding in your palm a computer that tracks your glowing golf ball at night. The course is dimly lit, as if from the light of a full moon, and your game is both visual and intuitive, as you rely on your inner guidance, backed by your electronic ability to track the ball. The course is built on a reclaimed landfill due to the scarcity of available property. But, never fear, the glow of your ball is healthy and not irradiated by the now hermetically sealed waste that used to fuel a nuclear device.

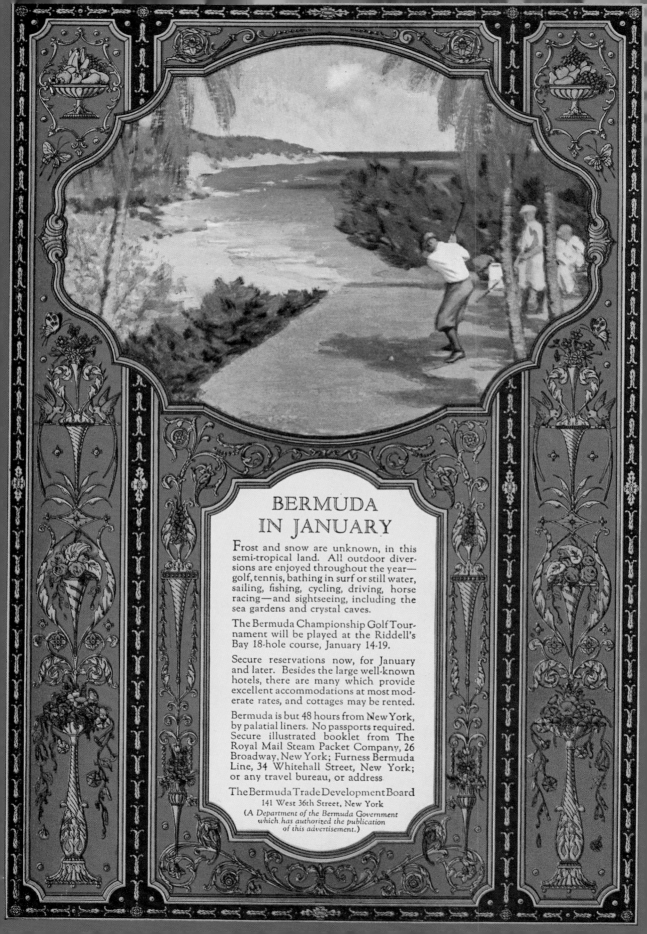

BERMUDA
IN JANUARY

Frost and snow are unknown, in this semi-tropical land. All outdoor diversions are enjoyed throughout the year— golf, tennis, bathing in surf or still water, sailing, fishing, cycling, driving, horse racing—and sightseeing, including the sea gardens and crystal caves.

The Bermuda Championship Golf Tournament will be played at the Riddell's Bay 18-hole course, January 14-19.

Secure reservations now, for January and later. Besides the large well-known hotels, there are many which provide excellent accommodations at most moderate rates, and cottages may be rented.

Bermuda is but 48 hours from New York, by palatial liners. No passports required. Secure illustrated booklet from The Royal Mail Steam Packet Company, 26 Broadway, New York; Furness Bermuda Line, 34 Whitehall Street, New York; or any travel bureau, or address

The Bermuda Trade Development Board
141 West 36th Street, New York
(A Department of the Bermuda Government which has authorized the publication of this advertisement.)

GETAWAY GOLF

Fortunately, there's a lot for a golfer to do when the usual routine gets boring, or bitter winter winds lift whorls from snowdrifts on the third green, or a muscle hurts too much to swing a club. Golf offers us many enjoyable golf-related activities when we are not actually golfing.

GOLF ON THE ROAD

Exploring new courses can be an adventure. A couple we know takes a two-week vacation with their clubs in the trunk. They drive to a course, play it, and ask for the names of other good courses up the road. They call ahead, book a tee time, and off they go to the next course. Another couple escapes the winter by getting AAA maps, aiming their motor home at the southwest, and playing courses all along the way.

Need advice on which courses to play? Look for books with titles that begin *Golf Courses of . . .* and give detailed descriptions, directions, green fees, and amenities for the places that interest you. For online information, go to your favorite search engine and type "golf" and the city, state, region, or country where you want to play. Or go to one of the online golf discussion groups (like rec.sport.golf) and ask, "Where should I play golf in Austin, Texas?" You'll get answers. Most golfers are friendly, helpful folks.

But why wait for vacation time to roll around? You can combine a day or weekend trip with golf. Going over the

Resort golf in Hawaii

river and through the woods to grand-mother's house? Start two and a half hours early and play nine holes along the way. Think of your golf outing as a mini-vacation. What a wonderful break, even if you only have time to play once a month. A vacation every month!

I'm a golf tourist and sightseer. Some golfers buy a house close to a course and play it for decades. They gain the intimate appreciation of a course that continuous play brings. Golf is always right outside or just a few blocks away. Some of us, on the other hand, like to explore courses that are new to us.

TOURIST GOLF

Some golfers set themselves a life-time goal to play in faraway places with strange-sounding names. Away from home, the courses seem familiar, but strangely so. Flags in holes in the greens? Check. Tees? Check. Bunkers? Roger that. Fairways? Check. But things seemed different, almost dreamlike when we played our first Florida course and heard the splashing and grunting of alligators in the water hazards. A new region offers different topography, vegetation, hazards, and animal life.

Here comes your golf geography lesson, so pay attention, class. We want your mouth to water, then we want you to hit the road.

"My favorite thing is to go where I have never gone."
—Diane Arbus

Links and seaside courses

A Scot, bred on true seaside links courses, would guffaw to see the names of courses with the word "links" paired with words like "mountain," "maple," "cedar," or other trees. Not all courses that call themselves "links" are true links courses. It takes sand, river estuaries, and undulating dune landscapes, ceaselessly formed and reformed by sea winds, to make a course a true links course.

What are their special natural features? These courses are open, with few trees or none, and few distinct hills as natural markers. There's you, golf, and oceanic spaces beyond. A certain amount of disorientation is associated with links play, requiring that a golfer get a feel for judging distances. Hidden swales and contoured rolling fairways are often deceptive, and sand bunkers can be invitingly soft and deep. The fairways, built on sandy, well-drained ground, are generally hard, so your ball loves to roll a long way.

Links courses are famous for their windy, wet playing conditions and unpredictable weather. The best strategy is to hit straight, low line drives. Your usual nine-iron shot might require a seven to go the same distance into the

Courtesy Bandon Dunes Golf Course, Bandon, OR

Ocean, sand, and wind shape the traditional links course at Bandon Dunes.

Courtesy Dave Werschkul

Pebble Beach Golf Course, one of the premier seaside courses in the world

wind, hence the phrase, "a two-club wind." Many golfers suggest hitting the ball so it rolls onto the green as opposed to hitting a high shot that risks being blown short or out of play.

When the wind blows, let go of your usual scoring expectations. "Bogey golf" seems like par, especially if you're playing in a gale. Tee the ball lower and swing easy to keep the ball low into the wind.

Links courses are designed along minimalist lines with few modifications to the natural seascape topography. There is something primeval and exciting about looking toward a mist-shrouded, emerald green framed by an angry, rolling sea, topped by white-capped waves. The smell of the ocean

invigorates the soul. You feel deeply the true spirit of old golf on a links course.

> **TIP:** Windbreakers, rain gear, and waterproof shoes are strongly suggested for these types of courses. Unless it's a cloudless sky, you'd better dress for all-weather golf on a links course.

Seaside courses are similar to links courses in their coastal location but differ in their inclusion of trees, water hazards, and a general parkland course look. Links courses are sited in dune formations. Typical seaside courses, however, have rock outcroppings that rest on the old sea terraces of rocky coastal headlands. They have the wind.

They have the rain. But they are not open like links courses. They play like a parkland course set along the sea.

Parkland courses

The first parkland-style courses were carved out of woods and orchards as golf began to migrate inland from its coastal beginnings. Because of the easy availability of water, designers incorporated water hazards into their courses. We have donated many a ball in gratitude.

Parkland fairways have a sweeping, rolling character. Trees, so noticeably absent on links courses, contribute to the scenic beauty and playing challenges. They offer reference points for positioning shots. Trees are also penalty hazards. Grasses are often lush and moist because of the high moisture content in the clay soils they grow on. Your ball gets a good lie perched up on those muscular grasses, but it rolls only a few yards after it lands, due to the soft ground. Winds swirl due to the patchwork of trees. Check their tops. They make good wind indicators.

"Where'er you walk, cool gales shall fan the glade;

Trees, where you walk, shall crowd into a shade."

—Alexander Pope, *Pastorals*

What else can I tell you about parkland courses? I was raised on parkland courses, so to me, they are the standard brand golf course. Anything else still looks exotic. You say "golf course," I think "parkland." My ball flies to trees like a homing pigeon.

Desert courses

Beware of the beautiful, shimmering desert course whose sun produces a chiaroscuro of light and shadow that distorts distance perception. Heat waves can create a mirage effect. Arid courses adjacent to mountains are especially fun to play because of the visual distortions and other perspective puzzles created by course designers.

Sandy desert soils create firm fairways and greens that cause the ball to bounce and roll farther on fairways. Putting surfaces vary from fast to lightning fast. Narrow, water-hungry fairways are bordered by true desert cacti.

Courtesy Pasatiempo Golf Course, Santa Cruz, CA

Pasatiempo, an historic links course designed by Alister MacKenzie, has evolved into a tree-lined parkland course.

A beautiful desert course at Cabo Real, Baja Sur, Mexico

The ball travels farther because of the thin, dry air. Many desert holes have raised greens and carries over arroyos. Dry washes are common, necessitating the use of a high loft wedge to land the ball softly and keep it from rolling down into a bristling cactus patch.

Respect the desert rough. Misjudged

"Picture this: a 429-yard-desert-course-par-4 hole with a wasteland-protected-dogleg-left-heavily-guarded green with bunkers so deep that if you stood in one, the green level was still five feet beyond your up-stretched hand. My third shot stuck and held while Rich and Dave stood below out of my sight in sandy chasms on opposite sides of the green. As I watched, from the rear up came Rich's sandblasting third shot, which lofted and headed for the right rough. Then, seeming to freeze in flight, it squarely hit the middle of the pin, seemed to stick, and dropped like a rock into the cup. Not a half second later, dumbfounded, I witnessed Dave's more traditional shot arch above the green, hit the putting surface, take one bounce, and roll in as if remote controlled. Only I had seen this miracle which I jubilantly recounted as they peered down disbeliev-ing into the cup."

—Wayne Schumacher, member of our OK Golf League

shots can lead to close encounters with a cactus, horned lizard, desert tortoise, and other wonderful desert creatures. There are no woodland roughs in the desert, but stands of Saguaro and Cardon cacti offer even more difficult, thorny personalities. These giant cacti cohabit with other spiny friends, including the jumping cholla, prickly pear, and the brawny barrel cactus. If you venture into these desert roughs to find your ball, you had better take combat boots, tin pants, and a long ball-retriever.

In some desert areas large springs surface, creating a green and magical oasis. Date and coconut palms sway over the green vegetation, the course seems a beautiful mirage, and a golfer lucky enough to play a desert course will treasure the memories.

TIP: Take water, sunscreen, sunglasses, and a wide-brimmed hat for protection. Hydration is important, so drink often to stay ahead of the heat and exhaustion curve.

Mountain courses

My Hoosier cousin visited us a few years back. After a long drive, making a big gesture with both her hands as if she were calling a runner safe, she said, "All day, I just wanted to smooth out all those damned mountains." Flatlanders are similarly challenged on mountain golf courses.

What fun. Golfing challenges spring up like mushrooms on mountain courses. Putts curve away from the hole in rainbow arcs. Drives and irons shots

Courtesy John R. Johnson

The Mountain Course at Incline Village with Sierra Nevada mountain backdrops

bounce once on a hill and also curve away in rainbow arcs. Be ready to play the break in fairway shots, just as you do on the greens, to end up where you want to be. Your lies can be uphill, downhill, all around the hill, with each lie demanding a novel adjustment to your stance. Oh yes, and elevated tees reduce the distances printed on the scorecards; elevated greens increase them.

Wild flowers, blooming late in summer mountain meadows, add to the beauty. Mountain courses can create a sense of golfing vertigo due to the steep terrain and dramatic landform changes. The atmosphere is thin at higher elevations, and a ball can travel up to 15% farther than at lower levels. At these higher elevations, you might have a higher heart rate and shorter breath for a few days until your body adjusts. Take it easy.

Dramatic changes in altitude, coupled with mountain gloom and mountain glory, create some of the best scenic courses golf can offer. Imagine teeing off down a slope carved by an ancient glacier that ends at the edge of a classic cirque or a glacier-carved lake. The alpine scenery draws you into the canyons and ridges and along the base of a mountain. Lateral and terminal moraines define the boundaries of mountain courses often sited in upland meadows, serenaded by musical brooks fed by snow runoff and crystal clear mountain springs.

TIP: Bring your camera and expect to take photographs that you will enjoy for a lifetime.

Beware of the coiled cobra.

Tropical courses

Lush vegetation and occasionally steep topography combine in tropical and subtropical courses. There golf is played in a warm, breezy paradise with brightly colored flowers and birds as regular visitors. Tall palm trees sway in trade winds mixed with the sounds and sights of crashing surf and white sand beaches. The air is thick with scent.

Many of the courses are designed to take advantage of the trade winds that blow steadily throughout much of the year. Humidity and the resulting dense vegetation can make it hard to find a ball out of bounds.

"A player may remove a ball two club lengths from a coiled cobra or sleeping tiger without penalty of death. He may also run like a scared jackrabbit."
—Robert Trent Jones,
Golf by Design

Courtesy Westin Mauna Kea Beach Hotel, Big Island, HI

Mauna Kea. Resort golf in a tropical Hawaiian paradise

in making a putt. Remember, a ball running with the grain will go faster than a ball putted against the grain. Afternoon rain in the tropics is a daily ritual which dampens the grass and softens the ground, cutting down on your distance.

TIP: To avoid heat exhaustion and discomfort it is best to play in the early morning or late afternoon. A light tropical shirt and shorts are recommended golf attire, and thick applications of sunscreen are suggested. Staying hydrated is a must for tropical golf.

THE GOLF PILGRIMAGE

"To Scotland: and conclud[e] in hearty prayers

That your attempts may overlive the hazard."
— Shakespeare,
Henry IV, Part II

Tropical grasses such as Bermuda grass, elephant grass, kuch grass, and zoysia are thick and, especially when the ball is nestled down into the grass, they produce a very difficult lie. The grain in these grasses is crucial to reading the green and will be a factor

If golf were a religion, Scotland would be the Holy Land. Once in a lifetime a true believer should make a pilgrimage to the shrines of modern golf. Think about a visit to St. Andrews, your opportunity to travel the path of deeper knowledge and gain additional insights and perspectives. The traditions of golf were

Courtesy Elizabeth Reid

Historic St. Andrews village

handed down to us as a treasure for our enjoyment and safekeeping. The Scottish game serves as a model for "golf as it should be played."

Scott's sister, Elizabeth, and brother-in-law, Charley, recently returned from a trip to St. Andrews and other parts of Scotland, and they brought back wonderful stories of their journey, adventures, and local hospitality. Not golfers themselves, they went in search of their Scottish roots, which are tied into the Scot clan, Scott's namesake. He is a descendent of Mary, Queen of Scots, who played golf soon after her husband was murdered. Elizabeth discovered that the family has a castle, a coat of arms, and a plaid

pattern for the clan. Scott was hoping for at least part ownership of a golf course but says he'll settle for a plaid kilt.

Most of Scotland, including the more remote regions, is accessible by train and bus. Accommodations are reasonable, as are meals and public transportation. Elizabeth brought back photographs, lots of maps depicting golf courses, golf books, and other memorabilia for us. The city of St. Andrews and surrounding towns and villages are quaint, beautiful, and full of their own rich history, golf notwithstanding. Elizabeth loved the antique shops and old bookstores and the Old World architecture.

RESORT GOLF

Want to saturate yourself in golf? Spend a few days to a week at a golf resort. Just decide what kind of golfing experience you want—easy, hard, exotic, a variety of courses. An all-day golf outing might net you 27 or 36 holes, perhaps a round on two different courses. You will play golf during the day and dream golf all night. We know of groups of 20 or more golfers who go on such outings annually and have a fine time.

We are not going to tell you how to book your flight or arrange your trans-portation once you are at your destination. You already know to ask for the "best rate," "weekly rates," "group rates," "family rates," and "specials" wherever you inquire. Just be aware that some resorts allow you to stay off the premises (when local motels and hotels become options); others require you to stay at the resort if you wish to play. Find out what kinds of packages

Courtesy Big Cedar Lodge Resort, Ridgedale, MO

are offered. Sometimes it's as inexpensive to stay and play on-site as to stay at a no-star motel away from the resort.

> **TIP:** If you are travelling with non-golfing family or companions, be sure there is enough to entertain them. When you contact the resort, inquire about the amenities, including non-golf and nighttime activities, shopping, and tourist opportunities.

You can reserve your stay yourself by going online or doing research in books or magazine ads and directories of resort courses. Ask around for recommendations among your golfing friends or at your pro shop. Or you might want to contact a golf tour company or local travel agent. Resorts also offer package deals that include airfare,

accommodations, confirmed tee times, prepaid green fees, cart rental, and all taxes. Group and tournament rates are often available. Just ask. Expect to spend anywhere from $100 to $250 or more per day, depending on whether you want a budget or posh golfing experience.

GOLF SCHOOLS

For learning more about the game and increasing your golfing skill, many opportunities for instruction exist. There are local clinics, run by club pros or visiting teaching professionals. If your group is large enough, you can invite a pro to give a group lesson. Or you can go away for a weekend or more, taking a learning vacation, and receive golf instruction in golfing fundamentals, etiquette, and course management. You will be going to school with people who want to be there and who walk, talk, eat, and sleep golf. It can be memorable.

There are co-ed schools and schools for women, men, juniors, seniors, business groups, beginning, and experienced golfers. There might be a regional school close to you offering lessons, or you can choose a residential school, usually providing accommodation, amenities, green fees, and social events with the instruction package. Ask your local pro for advice, or ask golfers who have gone to school about their experiences. For online information, type "golf schools" or "golf instruction" into a search engine.

Courtesy Elizabeth Reid

A tournament at St. Andrews

DOING TOURNAMENTS

Those who love the game often follow professional golf tournaments on television. My 87-year-old aunt says it's more relaxing than watching football. (My uncle can't watch the second half of any Notre Dame game, because of his heart. He gets too excited.)

The pros bring an exquisite form, confidence, and finesse to the game. When they are "in the zone," they seem able to will their shots. Watching them on television, we see a level of play that is the perfection of thought. A few years ago Davis Love III (Scott says I look like him) hit a shot against the hill in back of a green. It rolled back down and into the cup. It was no accident! *He played it that way.*

If you like to watch your favorite golfers on television, there's nothing like seeing the great players in person. Consider attending at least one professional tournament.

TIP: Go to a local tournament—high school, college, city, or state—just to get a feel for following the action. You'll learn a lot about how to watch a tournament. You'll be supporting your local golfers too. And local tournaments are a lot less expensive than professional ones.

Be a sitter

When you go to see professional golf at a tour event, decide whether you'll be a sitter, a walker, or both. If you want to see the thrills, chills, and spills around the 18th green, you should stake out your place early in the morning. You are betting that the outcome will be decided here. That's not always the case, but a tournament can be very exciting when it's won on the last hole.

The wait for the first group can be long, so bring your personal entertainment system—book, crossword puzzles, radio, and earphones. Except when the monitors request absolute quiet, you'll also be able to talk golf with your neighbors. Late in the day, when the contenders arrive, you will have tens of thousands of neighbors.

Think about your home course. Where would you watch a tournament on it? A course usually has a place where three or more holes converge. That's a good spot to be, since you can easily see lots of different shots. Another good location is at the green of a par 5 where you can observe the longest hitters try to get on in two, sometimes fail, and sometimes hit spectacular recovery shots. Study the course map to find these sites or, better, as soon as you arrive in the morning, walk the course backward, starting at the 18th, and size it up. It takes about one and a

half hours. It's good exercise, and you'll discover the best vantage points.

It's always fun to watch players warm up on the practice range and at the practice green doing chipping and putting. Note how many balls they hit before they step onto the first tee. How many do you hit (hint, hint) before you tee off? Note how loosely they hold their clubs, especially the putter. I remind myself they are cradling a baby bird in their hands, not strangling a snake.

Be a walker

If you walk, decide whether you want to follow a favorite player or grouping or see the field. Pick up the pairings sheet when you arrive to find out who is playing in which group and in what order. You might want to follow one group for a few holes and then follow another, just to see different players and playing styles.

Here's a suggestion for seeing the whole field hitting a variety of different shots. Position yourself at the first tee. Watch all the groups go off. Then move to the seventh or eighth fairway and watch all the groups hit fairway shots. Then

move to the 16th green and watch all the groups hit their approach shots and putt out. By the time the leaders move to the 18th tee, it will be too crowded to see much, but you will have seen a lot of the day's play. Next tournament, you can sit at the 18th green.

> **TIP:** Make a note of what kind and color clothes your favorites are wearing, so you can spot them at a distance when you are out on the course.

Make yourself comfortable

Unless you are there mainly to party hearty with the beautiful people in the celebrity tent, you are going to be out on the course for eight hours or more. Take a tip from the caddies— wear comfortable walking shoes. Take power snacks in case you can't find or don't like the dog-burger-fries fare. Take water.

Wear sunglasses and a hat. Slather on sun block unless you are collecting carcinomas along with players' autographs. Store rainwear, umbrella, and extra socks in your trunk. Carry a backpack or fanny pack with your essentials. Unless it's Sunday

when they run out of souvenirs, buy your mementos on the way out so you don't have to rent a donkey cart to haul them around.

Volunteer

Another way to experience a tournament is to volunteer your services. You might work admissions, the driving range, first aid, or leader boards. Or you could run the player shuttle, work in the scoring tent, be a marshal, or do one of the many other tasks. Maybe you'll be the one holding up the sign that says, "Quiet, please." You usually get a souvenir golf shirt as well as the best seat at a tee or a hole.

MILITARY GOLF—R&R

"Military golf" doesn't mean troops in fatigues jumping out of tanks and amphibious assault vehicles storming a course. Military courses

A more relaxed form of military golf is played today.

Early golf air commuters

Golf in the combat zone is nothing new. When Scott spoke to retired Navy Commander Al Stetz, he learned of golfers literally playing in Viet Nam combat zones, and Eric Yoder writes of a paratrooper who carried a golf club with him during the Normandy invasion of World War II. Sailors on board submarines practice their putting skills as a means of relieving boredom and tension.

If you are a taxpayer don't worry. U.S. military courses have been paid for long ago and do not depend on taxpayer dollars. In fact, income from user fees helps fund installation supported youth activities from childcare to teen centers as well as other outdoor recreational activities. Golf helps improve the quality of life of service personnel who, we firmly believe, are entitled to the same lifestyle and the same recreational opportunities that

were established to provide healthy recreation and a means of building "espirit de corps" within the armed forces. Courses act as pressure relief valves for the stress and rigors of military life, especially during times of war. Golf is a favorite activity for rest and relaxation, especially for personnel stationed overseas.

Numerous military courses are located in Taiwan, Germany, Japan, Korea, France, England, and other countries. Many were constructed around 1915 during World War I, and construction continued through World War II until the 1950s. General, later President, Eisenhower was an avid golfer who added to the popularity of golf in the military during the late '40s and '50s.

Golf in the danger zone

There is a story circulating in military circles about Desert Storm warriors who rolled and oiled desert sand to create "greens" and used artificial turf remnants to drive and hit fairway shots.

Shore leave in the country

Courtesy Fort Meade Public Affairs

Military golfer getting R&R

they are pledged to defend.

There is a popular misconception that golf is for officers only, but the courses are open to all ranks of active duty, military reservists, and retired personnel. Most military golfers sport mid and high handicaps. Many courses have a sliding scale of green fees based on rank, so a private pays less than a sergeant who pays less than a colonel. Scott's active duty discharge papers allow us to play a local Veterans Administration course, run and maintained by volunteers.

Base courses

Imagine teeing off next to a Marine Corps F-18 Hornet fighter about to engage the afterburner. The golfers at El Toro Marine Corps Air Station in Santa Ana, California, know this sound well and have grown accustomed to the roar and fumes of passing jets. Golfers at Guantanamo Bay, Cuba, are used to the idea of taking a piece of artificial turf with them to hit their shots from the barren sand and rock surfaces that exist between tee and green. Water is a scarce commodity on this U.S. Navy base and is utilized sparingly on just the tees and greens of this "Cold War" course.

The Air Force Academy course in Colorado Springs, Colorado, is spectacular with vistas of the Rocky Mountains in all directions. Another beautiful course is located at McChord

R&R in the far north

Air Force Base, near Seattle, Washington. This course looks on lush greens, graceful trees lining the fairways, and Mount Rainer towering in the background.

Where to play

Images of desert cactus, lofty mountains, swaying tropical palms, and ocean beach vistas are powerful incentives to play. Military personnel are no different than civilians in their desire to escape cold weather, olive drab surroundings, and the din of everyday existence. Military golf courses, like their civilian counterparts, tend to be concentrated in the South and in Arizona, California, and Hawaii. In addition, military courses are also located on remote and sometimes exotic places that can bring excitement to the military golfer seeking to expand geographical golfing experiences.

If you are in the military and looking for a special golf course experience, you

might want to try out the following courses: Fort Lewis, Washington (Army); McChord Air Force Base, Washington; Pearl Harbor, Hawaii (Navy); Camp Pendleton Marine Base, California; and Otis Coast Guard Station, Cape Cod, Massachusetts. Al Stetz gives five stars to them in his book, *In Search of Eagles*, a very useful reference on military courses.

ARMCHAIR GOLF

One way of taking pleasure from the sport is to let your imagination do the walking. We've already mentioned the televised competitive tours and the golf channel with its domestic and foreign tournaments, as well as tips, lessons, interviews, histories, biographies, and new developments in golf equipment. The springs of golf run deep and wide, and the sport has inspired writers. Here are some additional resources for enjoying golf under your own roof.

Golf books

These are our favorite books on golf-for-the-fun-of-it. They are not how-to books with improvement tips, not compilations of best courses, not biographies. These books express appreciation for the game and continual deep delight in it.

10) *Golf and the Spirit*, M. Scott Peck. This is a reflective examination of the psychological resources and lessons for life golf offers. Also worthy of mention for its thoughtful appreciation of the game is *Golf Beats Us All* by Joseph A. Amato.

9) *Mostly Golf: A Bernard Darwin Anthology*, Bernard Darwin. Darwin, grandson of Charles Darwin, is considered the greatest English golf essayist.

8) *Golf Dreams*, John Updike. Updike writes trenchant, thoughtful essays on golf.

7) *The Legend of Bagger Vance*, Steven Pressfield. Pressfield gives us a well-plotted account of an imaginary match held among Bobby Jones, Walter Hagen, and local southern golfer, Rannulph Junah. It's in somewhat the same vein as Michael Murphy's *Golf in the Kingdom*, another favorite.

6) *Golf Course Design*, Robert Muir Graves and Geoffrey S. Cornish. This book is an outstanding overview of the historical, aesthetic, and technical aspects of golf course architecture.

5) *The Anatomy of a Golf Course*, Tom Doak. A contemporary, young golf course architect, Doak gives us an insider's view of golf course design and hints about the future of golf.

4) *Extraordinary Golf: The Art of the Possible*, Fred Shoemaker. He writes well on the freedom and happiness available to golfers who are willing to understand the difference between performance (low score) and purpose (personal growth and fulfillment).

3) *Five Lessons: The Modern Fundamentals of Golf*, Ben Hogan, and Herbert Warren Wind. Yes, we know, it's about lowering your score, but it's also about golf seen through the eyes of one of the best golfers and golf writers and a classic of its kind.

2) *Missing Links* by Rick Reilly. This is a sometimes hilarious account of class warfare between what we call Golf, Esq. and muni golf.

And our number one golf book is

1) *The Golf Omnibus,* by P.G. Wodehouse. This book is our absolute favorite: a collection of golf stories by a comic genius who knew and loved golf and the English language equally.

GOLF COLLECTIBLES

Another way of enjoying golf when it's too dark, rainy, or cold to play is to collect it. Golf has a long material history because golfers have thrown off so much impedimenta in the 600 or more years since the Scots devised their peculiar pastime. And most of the artifacts of the sport have been fashioned with meticulous craftsmanship.

"To select well among old things is almost equal to inventing new ones."
—Nicolas Charles Trublet

I happen to think that woods, the ones formerly made out of wood, are wonderful to look at and hold. Wooden-shafted clubs also feel good to the touch. But who knows, our great-grandchildren may grow misty-eyed and reckless when at auction they pursue the graphite-shafted metal-woods that we take for granted. To have and to hold, to show and to share, these are the pleasures of collecting things golf.

Dealers and online auctions offer golfing art and memorabilia for sale, and you can also find them at golf shows and expositions. For the hunters and gatherers among us, there are a Golf Collectors Society and a British Golf Collectors Society, regional collectors' organizations, antique price guides, newsletters. You can spend big money (tens of thousands of dollars for a featherie in fine condition), little money (golf caps and balls), or no money (monogrammed pencils and scorecards from the courses you play), depending on what you fancy.

Here are some of the multitudes of things that golf collectors do fancy:

Equipment: antique and vintage clubs, putters, balls, tees, bags, clothes
Art: paintings, lithographs, posters, prints, ceramics, glassware, silverware
Tournament collectibles: scorecards, trophies, medals, badges
Games: toys, puzzles, board games, playing cards, poker chips
Books and periodicals: by or about famous golfers and courses; club histories
Ephemera: postcards, matchbooks, advertisements, cigarette cards
Stamps: golf on stamps, which constitutes a recognized topical area for collectors

Courtesy Golf Tours, International

Golf at Mission Hills Resort, Shenzhen, China

TIP: If you collect golfiania, remember it's condition, condition, condition. Original state, *not* refinished, is more desirable. (Don't sand or polish the patina and stains off your prize!) Also, the more rare, usually the more desirable and the more expensive.

COURSE COLLECTING

If you have been extraordinarily fortunate in your choice of investments, inventions, or inheritance, you will be able to buy or build golf courses that stretch like a jade necklace across vast spaces. Otherwise, you'll have to collect courses by playing them. Consider setting yourself a long-term goal of playing many different ones. Scott wants to play every course built by Alister MacKenzie, his favorite architect. I'd like to play the odd course, the whimsical, the bizarre, eccentric, and far away.

Consider drawing up a list of courses you want to play over your golfing career, your golf "life list." You might choose to play a certain number of the 100 best courses in the country, or all the courses on the PGA tour, all the courses in your state, courses in each geographical region, the oldest course in each state or country you visit, or play golf on every continent. Perhaps you will find more satisfaction in realizing this kind of golfing goal than breaking some arbitrary score.

THANK YOU FOR THE MEMORIES

You might want to collect your memories. They're inexpensive, and they're yours. Some golfers keep their scorecards as a record of the courses they have played. The date is recorded, perhaps the signatures of playing partners, and those cards are then filed in boxes, put in scrapbooks, or scanned into an image archive or onto a web page. The woman Scott bought his clubs from had a collection of ball markers from every course she played.

A sports journal or diary is a useful

"Getaway golf" can mean autumn golf on a course you usually play in summer.
Quail Point Golf Course, Medford, Oregon

addition to your enjoyment of the game. We've mentioned bird watching and personal course rating as subject matter for your entries, but you might include golf jokes you've heard, greens hit in regulation, or whatever your particular interest is. The journal becomes your inner scorecard, used to keep track of what matters most to you during a round. I've seen racks mounted on a wall with balls sporting course logos from each course this golfer played. This was his personal golfing record. Another golfer we know collects monogrammed golf hats from his favorite courses.

A camera can preserve your favorite holes, your playing partners, some scenic vista or surprising event. You can keep your favorite pictures in a golf album or archived in your computer and sent to people who enjoy golfing scenes.

"Go out and see for yourself. Make others see what you've seen."
  —Eleanor Roosevelt

If you are of the artistic persuasion, a photo can be the basis of a sketch, watercolor, or painting done during the golfless doldrums. When completed, you can hang them on your wall, give them to your golfing partners, friends, and family, or donate them to charity.

Whether you use photographs or written notes, keeping a record helps to increase your enjoyment of your game.

Golf into art

You focus on the specifics that make a round satisfying, and you remember the good parts.

WORLD GOLF

We have spoken to people who want to play a course on every continent, or every course a favorite architect built, or every course in their state. Why not set a lifetime goal for your own golf career? The world is your golf course, and you have the rest of your life to play it.

MARCH   1900   TEN CENTS

THE LADIES' HOME JOURNAL

8

A L T E R N A T I V E
G O L F

"One's destination is never a place but rather a new way of looking at things."
—Henry Miller

There's no reason to restrict golf to a golf course, available tee times, and summer weather. Golf is a state of mind; golf is where you find it or how you make it. We've met people who play in all sorts of places and all sorts of ways, reinventing the game in the process. The genie of golf will not be confined to a "regulation" course.

MOON GOLF

In February of 1971 Apollo 14 astronauts spent 33.5 hours on the moon. As a result of this mission two golf balls currently rest on the moon's surface. One is in the lunar dust. The second is in the hole, if a crater two miles in diameter can be called a hole. If I ever get to the moon, I will look around for the balls, but for now I'm satisfied just knowing they are up there.

Those balls got to the moon in the true spirit of golf for the fun of it. Alan Shepard, commander of the Apollo 14 mission, was inspired to hit a ball on the moon by Bob Hope, whom Shepard and Deke Slayton took on a tour of NASA. Hope had brought a club along, which he was swinging around the NASA campus, and when he tried out the moon walker, he used the club to balance himself. That was all Shepard needed to begin planning his round of lunar golf.

The moonclub

Shepard had a 6-iron club head designed that would snap onto a tubular utility handle, a "contingency sample return," made of an aluminum alloy and principally used to gather dust and rock samples. Shepard practiced on earth, learning to swing his special 6-iron one-handed since he could not use a two-handed grip in the clumsy, pressurized space suit. He got clearance from the flight controller to hit two golf

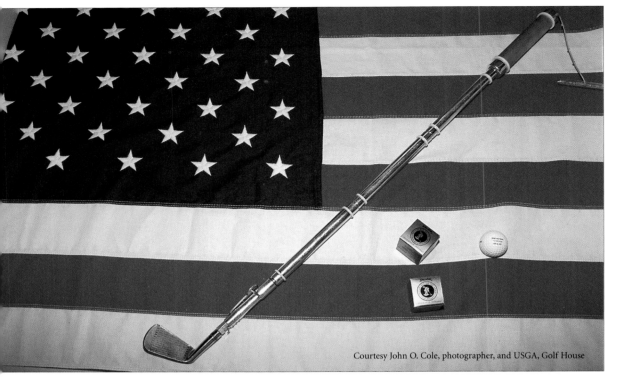

The 6-iron Shepard carried there and back

balls just before taking off from the lunar surface, but only if the mission had been safely completed. When it had been, he hit away.

A round of moon golf

First he tried what he called "a little sand-trap shot." He whiffed once, and then topped it a few feet on the second try. But with the third swing Shepard says he "made good contact" and hit the ball over 200 yards with a hang time of about 30 seconds in the 1/6 earth's gravity environment.

Excited by his success, he over-swung on his fourth try and shanked the second ball into a nearby crater about 40 yards away. "Miles and miles," he said with astronaut irony. He folded the club up, carried it on board, and brought it back to the earth. Currently it awaits the next round of moon golf in the USGA Museum in, appropriately enough, Far Hills, New Jersey. And wasn't it fitting, considering theories of the pastoral origins of the game, that a man named Shepard intro-duced golf to the Moon People?

If we are going to colonize space, it is right and proper to carry our games with us. We take our technology, so why not our spirit of play, the bedrock of human culture? *Homo ludens* should be up there alongside *homo techne*. And what better way to exercise after a long flight in cramped quarters than playing

Alan Shepard with club and moon golf cart

moon golf. What better way of exploring a lunar mare than fluffing up a golf ball in the lunar dust.

WINTER GOLF

The assumption that golf is a summer sport is an unfortunate one if it confines our play to the months with no "r" in them when temperatures soar and crowds of golfers, on public courses, at least, can slow play to a crawl. You feel like you're watching grass grow.

We've already told you how invigorating fall and spring golf can be. Now consider lowering your personal "threshold temperature" further, to 50, 40, 30 . . . degrees. Go out *winter golfing* to beat the winter blahs. Try it. If you are able, play at least a few rounds during the winter. (And I'm talking about playing in the snow, not moving south or taking a trip to warm-weather winter golf.) An added bonus to snow golf is that winter green fees go down or even disappear.

Winter golf is a whole new game. The course plays differently. When the ground is hard, you get more roll. A frozen water hazard can give you surprising distance. When the course is sodden, high lofted balls "plug," i.e., bury themselves, so you want to hit low shots. Because footprints on frozen greens can damage the grass, some courses establish temporary, winter greens for play. On them you get the flavor of the old, roughshod Scottish courses of centuries ago.

Design a snowshoe course

All it takes is a little imagination to make a snow golf course.

> **Tips** for constructing a snow golf course:
> 1) Buckets or coffee cans can serve as holes, or simply mark out generous areas as "holes" and be liberal with "gimmes."
> 2) Homemade flags can be made out of dowels and rags.
> 3) Food-coloring water can mark "greens." The crustier the snow, the better, but you can get by in just about any kind of snow.

Winter golf 100 years ago as captured by artist A.B. Frost

4) Consider using rubber balls, which will be easier to find, give you more roll, and plug in soft ground less often.
5) Consider using cross-country skis or snowshoes.
6) Keep the holes short the first time out, so you only have to carry a mid-iron and something to chip into the "hole" with.

Don't restrict possible venues to golf courses, though. If you are ambitious, you can put together a "Snow Golf Tourney" at a local ski area. Participants can buy a lift ticket up and then ski, snowshoe, or snowboard down the mountain, playing the holes as they go. One event we know of gives prizes for longest drive, closest to the pin, worst score, and best winter golf outfit. An après-golf, 19th-hole party with awards, videos, and the usual great golf stories can follow the event.

"Life shrinks or expands in proportion to one's courage."
— Anaïs Nin

A one-hole tournament

As an inspiring example of golf triumphing over climate, take the Annual Pillar Mountain Golf Classic in Kodiak,

Courtesy: Kodiak Daily Mirror

Winter golfers on top of the world

Alaska. This charity event is a par 70, *one-hole* snow golf tournament that goes up a mountain. Participants shoot 1400 yards up to the hole, a 5-gallon bucket sited on a snow-dyed "green" at the top of Pillar Mountain. A caddy and a spotter, whose job it is to keep track of the yellow or orange ball, accompany each golfer. Besides golf clubs, they may help their golfer carry a saw, hatchet, and shovel to provide playable lies in the alder thickets and gullies, including the fearsome "Ravine of Doom." PGA rules generally apply, but a local five-stroke penalty is assessed for waking a hibernating bear.

> **Tip**: Thin snow and crusty snow make the best surfaces to hit off.

Winter golf know-how

If you are going to play Polar Bear Golf, do it right. Here's what you need:

Feet: Warm feet make a happy outing. Wear wool socks and whatever footwear will keep you upright while you swing. Practice in your gear before going out to the "course."

Hands: I like gloves with inserts, so I can take off the outer glove for the swing. Or buy a pair of winter golf gloves for when it's not so cold. Hand-warmers can be helpful.

Clothes: I also like a hooded windbreaker over wool sweaters. Layer your clothes, since temperatures can change and exercise will warm you. Neck-warmers and earmuffs help too.

Drinks: No booze. I learned this watching Viking football outdoors in Minneapolis. Alcohol makes you colder. Take a thermos of hot coffee, chocolate, or tea.

Balls: Colored golf balls help. But you can also find your ball by tracking its footprints in the snow. When distances between bounces get shorter, you're getting closer. Take different makes of balls out since they will perform differently in cold weather.

Body piercings: Take them off or out. Metal conducts cold and hastens frostbite.

"Back in the '50s, five of us regularly played golf during the winter in Chicago. It was so cold, the balls would sometimes crack. We painted the balls orange so we could find them. Wind swept the snow from the fairways and pushed it up in drifts along the roughs. This one guy weighed all of 100 pounds, but he was the best tile layer in Chicago and had powerful wrists and forearms. He could really hit the ball. Once he climbed up on a drift after a ball, hit it, and sank up to his neck. He won all the bets, so we had a rule that the winner bought lunch. We played in really adverse conditions, but that was some of the best golf I ever played."
— Bill Chesney

XTREME GOLF

Want to combine a quick round of golf with a runner's aerobic workout? Wait, don't laugh. You can play a game

Aerobic golf

Courtesy Simone Garlaund

with aiming, a kind of golfing biathlon. The motto is: Grip it, hit it, and run like hell. The advantages for the runner in you are the beautiful settings and the soft running surface. The advantages for the golfer in you are a quick round of golf and an aerobic workout.

Getting on a course

Xtreme golf is still not widely known, so that chances are if you want to play you will probably have to get permission. Tell the pro that you'll be around the 18-hole course in an hour or so. You'll abide by their decision on green fees, dress code, days, and times. Because you will play so much faster than "slow golf" players, you will need to arrange a special time. Early mornings are the best so as not to interfere with other golfers. You'll be making first tracks in the morning dew. Assure the pro that if it works out, you will bring your golfing/running friends.

Xtreme equipment

Wear baggy shorts to carry your tees and a fanny pack for extra balls. The fewer clubs the better. A driver and 3-wood, a mid-iron, a pitching wedge, and a putter. A good way to carry your clubs is the Caddymate® or one of those old lightweight canvas bags. Some Xtreme golfers use a single club, usually an iron they hood for distance and putting.

of "Xtreme Golf," also called "speed golf," "running golf," or "fitness golf." This game combines fitness and skill. You run the course as you play. Putts are hit with the pin in. You score the game by adding your score to your running time. Lowest total score wins. Thus, if you play/run a nine-hole, par-36 course, shooting 45 in 40 minutes, your score is 85. In tournaments, stroke score is your net score, i.e. you deduct your handicap from your score before you add in your time.

"Whenever I draw a circle, I immediately want to step out of it."
— R. Buckminster Fuller

Xtreme golf is for you if you are a runner. You can do it jogging or cross-country racing, alone, with a running partner, or in highly competitive tournaments in which you combine speed

BACKYARD GOLF

My father told me that in the '40s, my maternal grandfather plowed up his front yard. The neighbors were dismayed, thinking he would plant corn or some other cash crop. He didn't. He planted bent grass. He had seen a green at a local course and decided he wanted a lawn that looked like that. So he brought a 2' x 2' square of creeping bent grass back from a friend in Detroit, cut it into little strips, and planted the yard. Each day, he watered it before he went to work at Studebaker's and after he came home.

By midsummer, he had a bent grass lawn, which he weeded and mowed close every other day. People would stop their cars, get out, and run their hand over that green carpet he had woven. Whether anyone ever putted that surface doesn't matter. It's enough for me to know that our family once owned a putting green for the sheer beauty of it.

"…a green thought in a green shade."
—Andrew Marvell, *The Garden*

More people today are building a practice/playing facility on their property. In places where courses are crowded or scarce, backyard golf is an answer. Because golf takes time away from home, it might be well worth the money to a young family to have a golf recreation area near at hand. The advantage of a backyard "course" is that it gives you an opportunity to practice at home and to play with friends and family.

If you like to garden and landscape, backyard golf might be a great hobby for you. You can install it yourself or with professional help, maintain it yourself or hire someone to maintain it for you. However you do it, you'll have golf available seconds from your door. Here are some specific backyard golf options:

Barebones backyard golf

If you want to start simple, try this if you have a backyard. Mow your lawn

A seaside quicksand trap

Herman and Sylvia's backyard driving range

and put a can approximately 4.25 inches in diameter into the ground. A flag, either a full-sized one or a small landscaping flag, can serve as your target, with or without the cup. If space is limited, you will probably want to use plastic practice balls so you don't hole out in one of your windows.

Our friends Herman and Sylvia have a driving range that will accommodate shots with lofted woods. They built a driving platform/tee box and aim at a tire in a fenced paddock about 150 yards away. If the ball goes too short they lose it in the blackberries; too long, and it's in the creek beyond.

Personal putting green

Depending on the space you have available, you can construct your own putting green, maybe with a sand bunker or two. If you want more information, call local golf course

superintendents. You might be able to contract with one to oversee construction and maintenance. Or contact landscaping companies to see whether one will build you a green. Drainage, grass diseases, and maintenance can be tricky and give you real headaches if not done right. A synthetic turf putting green, one that more or less resembles the feel of real grass greens, makes a much more easily maintained putting surface.

> **TIP**: If you have a young family, combine your green with a playground area so you and your children can be outdoors playing together.

For do-it-yourselfers, conduct an on-line search for "how to construct a green." Enterprising homeowners, using old reel push mowers set to cut at 3/8 of an inch, can construct usable greens for hundreds of dollars, not the tens of thousands it takes for constructing greens up to USGA standards. You might want to settle for greens that will help golfers work on their short games, get kids interested in golf, and contribute to mental health and family life. You can buy cups, flags, and hole cutters from golf course supply companies. Your local golf course superintendent is a good resource.

> **TIP**: A great reference for this project is *Backyard Putting Green Construction Manual*, by Leo Melanson.

Backyard golfers

Courtesy Jason Moss

The one-or-more hole course

If you have the space available, you might choose to build a par-3 or par-4 hole. Figure on tens of thousands of dollars for a professionally designed hole, less if you have time, landscaping expertise, and several green thumbs. If you have significant acreage, you can construct multiple holes. Two greens, adjacent tees, and parallel fairways will give you an out-and-back golfing experience. Three holes, with three different tee boxes aimed toward each hole, played three times will give you a tolerable nine-hole "round." One person we've heard of used two acres to site four par-3 holes, each of which had two sets of tees.

Costs of your private golfing preserve can vary from virtually zero, to millions of dollars, depending on whether you lay out your own chipping area on your existing yard or pay someone to design your own private 18-hole course.

SLAB CITY GOLF

Imagine a golf course that looks like the setting of Desert Storm. The landscape is stark and vast with barren mountains looming in the distance through shimmering heat waves. From a hilltop you can just make out the shapes of an odd assortment of trailers, buses, motor homes, and dune buggies. Wind generators, solar panels, antennas, and satellite dishes are mounted on the roofs of these vehicles. Military jets and helicopters fly over the desert beyond, dropping bombs and rockets to the chorus of Marine Corps artillery blasting away on the Chocolate Mountains Gunnery Range. Welcome to Slab City, California.

Suburban Slab City

The cold-weather refugees of the "Slabs" (so-called because of the cement foundation remnants of this decommissioned Marine Corps base) resemble a band of gypsies traveling and camping in their RVs. Some of the

Utopian desert golf community

Nadine Anglin, who gave them a tour of Gopher Flats Golf Course, the heart of Slab City golf.

Gopher Flats Golf Course

The course was designed and built in 1993 by Bob and Nancy Unden with lots of help from their neighbors and friends at Slab City. They were motivated because they were bored with just hitting golf balls into the desert. Alister MacKenzie would have been proud of their natural abilities to envision a course layout that required minimal earth moving and no removal of native creosote brush and other vegetation.

"On the human chessboard, all moves are possible."
— Miriam Schiff

The design principle was simple: "Find flat areas for the greens and fairways with not too many bushes or rocks." They started with three holes, then three more, then three more and, lo, a nine-hole course. All the raking, smoothing, and rock removal was courtesy of Slab City volunteers. The greens' flags were hand stitched by the women of the community.

The course is all par-3s with 1058 total yards. This is not a course for the

snowbirds look quite prosperous with motor homes and trailers that would interest a wealthy desert sheik, whereas others resemble caravans escaping from the dust bowl.

The common goal is the campsite at Slab City. The "Slabs" have everything a snowbird refugee from winter could want: warm desert climate, rent-free living, wide-open spaces, good companions, unlimited adventure, and, yes, "free golf." During winter, the population of Slab City includes 2000 free spirits in over 850 RVs. They camp side by side and join around evening campfires to share desert experiences. They tend to their own sick and donate food and sometimes money to those down on their luck.

Scott and his son Isaac were returning from a short vacation break in Mexico and decided to stop off at Slab City and research a true people's golf course. A fierce Santa Ana windstorm did not deter them, and they found

Isaac on ninth tee

GOPHER FLATS

GOLF
GOPHER
FLATS

A Bob Unden Course

Just minutes from . . .

SLAB CITY

	1	2	3	4	5	6	7	8	9	tot
	154	130	103	111	115	120	90	115	120	1058

Parking area

timid who don't like rocks dotting the fairway. If you decide to play, take along your old clubs that can withstand some more dents and dings. When Scott and Isaac played, the booming of distant guns made the experience even more memorable.

The tee boxes are built up slightly with raked sand and are defined by two fashionable truck tires, painted white, with yardage written on each tire. A rock-lined path ushers the golfer from green to next tee. Views from the tees include striking vistas of the Chocolate Mountains, the surrounding desert, and the Salton Sea in the distance. Most players walk the course, enjoying the exercise, but some pull a golf cart while others drive around in solar-powered carts that resemble vehicles in futuristic survivor movies.

Fairways are narrow strips of hard sand lined on both sides by creosote brush, cactus, and rocks. The natural desert provides all the hazards a golfer could wish for. The entire course is a giant sand bunker. Greens are natural sand, raked to playable conditions, much like the old-fashioned rolled sand "greens." Cups are approximately eight inches in diameter, about double regulation size. After putting, players are

Studying wind direction at Slab City

retriever caddy, Lily, for a quick game of Slab City golf.

They thoroughly enjoyed the challenging desert conditions, especially the sand greens, with their coffee can cups. This was free-form golf at its best. Isaac recently asked Scott if they could play a real course. We might have another future golfing buddy thanks to this alternative golfing experience.

5-IRON GOLF

One professional man in our town used to travel extensively as part of his consulting business. He was often invited to play by his clients. He liked to play golf on the road but not to lug his 14-club bag through airports and hotels. He decided to take charge of his game.

"The simple things give me ideas."
— Joan Miro

reminded to "smooth the greens" with the rug remnants available at each green.

As of this writing, the course is being expanded to 18 holes. Volunteers are getting ready with rakes, shovels, and wheelbarrows. Slab City vagabonds have created a course in the true spirit of golf for the fun of it. Credit card is not spoken here.

Conversion experience

Scott told me that this "weird" desert settlement and its odd golf course intrigued his teenaged son Isaac. He found an assortment of golf balls under one of the tire tee markers and, unprompted, picked up one of the short irons Scott had brought and began hitting balls from the tee box. Scott was surprised, since Isaac had steadfastly refused all earlier offers to play, and he quietly joined Isaac and their golden

He chose his favorite club—a 5-iron—and decided he would master its secrets in order to play one-club golf. For several days he went to the practice range and hit nothing but the 5-iron. He learned how to drive, chip, hit sand shots, and putt with that one club.

When traveling, he would carry his club onto the plane as a walking stick and store it in the oversized luggage area onboard. When he went to a course, he was greeted with amusement sometimes, occasionally with skepticism, other times with overt hostility. If his playing partners grumbled, he would say, "Look. Let me play two holes with you. If you don't like my game after that, I'll go back with no hard feelings." He told me that he never was sent back.

His sand shots were wristy. He learned to putt accurately by blading his putts. He could drive off a tee about 170 yards and hit about 160 from fairways, so at the end of two shots, he was usually out about 330 yards—and always in the fairway. He didn't mind taking a few more shots per round playing with just one club. "More bang for the buck," was his philosophy.

One person's trash

Once, a pro at a club the 5-iron golfer had played the previous year came up to him as he was checking in.

"I've been waiting for you. I've got a 5-iron I'd like you to try. Play with it for this round."

He did and liked it. Beautifully balanced, good shaft, a great feel.

"Nice club," he told the pro. "How much?"

"Fifty dollars to you. It's worth over $200. One of our members threw it in the lake, and I fished it out. He didn't want it back, so I've been saving it for you."

"Thanks, I'll take it."

He had the club regripped way down the shaft, so he could choke up for those delicate flip shots around the green. Actually, from the accounts he gave, he enjoyed *performing* his golf game. People like that are a menace to "serious" golf, but they are the models of golf for the fun of it.

Wilderness golf

Imagine playing on a course that is designed in such minimalist terms that it mirrors the surrounding natural landform and vegetation. Tees are sited on naturally elevated tops of hills. Narrow fairways follow the slope contours, ridges, and edges of the scrub oak and pine. Greens nestle into hills and rolling grass terraces. Hazards protecting the greens and defining the fairways consist of oak-Savannah thickets that tend to gobble up errant shots. Rock outcrops and steep slopes draw the ball like a magnet into the abyss below that is covered by thick vegetation and rocks. The occasional rattlesnake basking on the rocks or the coyote viewing your game from a distance adds to the flavor.

This is a wilderness course drawn lightly over the top of a working cattle

Scott hits a brave shot near a cow patty.

ranch in southern Oregon. The grazing cattle help to control the brush and keep the grass short. Cow pies represent a real course hazard, but you do get to move the ball if your shot lands in one. The game becomes "cowboy golf" when the course is played on horseback with the horse doing double duty as cart and caddy.

The main object is to have fun with a game that is more like the original form of golf played in Scotland, where mother nature created the course and the hazards. People who played this course have said, "This is the most fun I've ever had playing golf."

NIGHT GOLF

Interested in driving at night? Here are a couple of your options.

Land of the midnight putt

You can play summer golf in Norway, Sweden, Northern Scotland, Alaska, and Canada during summer months all day and most of the night. Dawson City in the Yukon, Canada, for instance, has almost 22 1/2 hours of daylight in June. For the other hour and a half, just sleep through the night.

Moonlight golf

Just can't get away to polar regions? Here are two other alternatives:

Night Courses: Some areas have courses, usually short, nine-hole courses, that are illuminated all or part of the night. The obvious advantages of playing at night are that it's a lot cooler and the wind dies down. If you're a young family, you can take the kids. If you're a very young family, you can get a baby sitter and play in the middle of the week.

Glow-in-the-dark Golf: It's 11 p.m. Do you know where your ball is? Yes, you do, if it glows in the dark. There are two types of bright balls to choose from. One is a hollow-core ball that uses a glow-stick insert. The other is a ball with a phosphorescent cover. The first kind keeps its charge, but it doesn't go as far as a regular ball. For best results, the second has to be frequently recharged with a light source (flashlight, UV light), but plays like a regular golf ball. Glow lights mark tees, fairways, hazards, greens, flag sticks, cups, and players, and carts are marked with glow lights.

For safety's sake, water holes and narrow, dangerous routings are often not played. When we practiced night golf, we found that the darker it was, the easier to track and find balls. We thought that for a tournament, it probably would be better to play from the front tees and limit the clubs to 5-irons and higher, just to make sure that the balls could be tracked and found. Fairways would have definitely have to be marked with glow lights and golfers would have to wear glow lights to keep track of each other. You are not going to shoot a career round at night, but it would be fun.

Night golf makes a great charity fundraising event, just because of the novelty. It's also a good way to end a daylong business conference at a golf resort. Courses like it as a way of bringing in more revenue or of providing a social evening for members of golf clubs.

It can be run with nine holes of regular golf played before twilight, a pause for supper, and nine or fewer holes played at night. Or you can do a pre-golf cookout and then swing all night. In our area, kids and adults play night golf on Halloween in costumes.

GOLF YOUR WAY

But enough of what we think about golfing for the fun of it. In the final chapter you'll see how other people play a relaxed, enjoyable brand of golf—golf their way. The more we talked to them, the more they convinced us that they've expanded the potential of the game. They've made it fit their stage of life, their temperaments, their needs. They've taken personal possession of the game of golf.

Courtesy Dave Werschkul

Golf is now 24/7.

A TASTEFUL GOLFING-GOWN.

"At first,
the infant"

"All the world's a stage, And all the men and women merely players; They have their exits and their entrances, And one man in his time plays many parts, His acts being seven ages."

—Shakespeare,
As You Like It

"Last scene
of all"

"The schoolboy"

"The sixth age
shifts"

"And then
the lover"

"Then a soldier"

"And then,
the justice"

A SPORT FOR
A LIFETIME

"The golfer is never old until he is decrepit. So long as Providence allows him the use of two legs active enough to carry him around the green, and of two arms supple enough to take a 'half swing,' there is no reason why his enjoyment in the game need be seriously diminished."
—Earl Balfour, *Golf*

Balfour was right. Golf is a sport for a lifetime, for women and for men. We can start very young and play well into old age. Obviously, we play a different game at 10 than we do at 30, 50, or 80, but it's always golf and it can always be enjoyable.

Up until now, you've read about the various ways people can have fun playing golf. Now, we want you to hear golfers speak in their own voices about why and how they enjoy the game. Their stories come from interviews we've conducted around the country. These are stories from the heart.

Throughout the book, we've borrowed liberally from Shakespeare from time to time. We're going to use the "Seven Ages of Man" passage from his play *As You Like It* to frame the interviews in this chapter. His words portray the circle of life that we've seen on golf courses. The "seven ages" are not strict categories. Younger golfers can be quite judicious and older golfers quite childlike in their delight in the game. Shakespeare helps us make the point that golf is for all people of all ages and all walks of life.

AT FIRST, THE INFANT

Children are always excited to learn. They take pride in imitating adults or older siblings. And when they play with a younger person,

"At first, the infant"

older golfers can rediscover the game by seeing it again through a child's eyes.

Camille's story

Six-year-old Camille and her mother visited our family one Thanksgiving. Camille told us she played miniature golf, so we took her out to the course the next day for some practice on the putting green. We said we were sorry we didn't have the right sized putter for her, but she said that was okay; she would borrow ours. She told us several times she was no beginner and knew how to hold a club. Afterwards she sent us an account of the outing, along with a drawing. She wrote, "I likt gofing. It was fan. I ded not got tird. I likt the balls."

Visualizing the shot

THEN THE SCHOOL BOY

We extend this next stage to include children and teens from about 11 to 17 years old. Athletic abilities are fairly well developed in boys and girls of this age. They are amazingly flexible and able to concentrate more on their shots. Many middle and high school programs offer golf as an elective and team sport for boys and girls.

Hanna Werschkul

Hanna is now 13. She used to play more golf when she was younger, but has not played much for the last couple of years. She told us she is going to take

On the practice green

"The schoolboy"

golf lessons this summer, and she thinks that she will enjoy playing more golf with her father, after she has developed additional golfing skills.

When did you begin playing golf?

When I was pretty young, around 8 years old. I went with my dad. I started putting, and that was fun. Then just being together and helping to carry the golf bag sometimes kept me going. I got clubs for Christmas, not a full set but some irons, a putter, and woods. After I got the clubs I started playing more golf with my dad. He gave me pointers on how to hold the club, swing at the ball, and stuff like that. My dad really loves to play golf, and I just wanted to be with him and play for fun.

A father and daughter game

Is there a story that you would like to share?

Once, I was playing with my dad and brother, and I was trying to keep up by hitting the ball two or three times. All of a sudden I heard a voice over the loudspeaker saying, "Will the little girl on the fairway please move aside so the following group can play though." Oh, are they talking about me? I thought. I was shocked by the loud voice, and I didn't know what to do. We went up to the golf office and my dad explained that we were just learning and they let us start again and I played faster.

Courtesy Jennifer Donohue

Adam Skibinski
How did you get started playing golf?

I'm 12 years old and when I was 10 my dad asked me if I wanted to play golf with him. I used my mom's old clubs, which we had shortened so that I could use them. My mom and dad took me to the driving range and they gave me some pointers on grip, plac-

ing my feet, swinging the club, and other stuff. Later on I took golf lessons at the Foxborough Golf Club with my friends. I like to play but I don't like to compete.

What attracted you to the game?

I really liked being able to hit the ball in the air and get to the green. Sometimes I would take out my anger about not hitting the ball good by hitting the ball real hard, but when I did that, I lost my focus and couldn't play well. I like just being outside with my family and friends. I love to feel the breeze, smell the grass, listen to the birds, and just like being in nature.

Patrick Oropallo's story

Patrick's mother is a single mom and has raised Patrick by herself, with no real "father figure" in his life. When Patrick started playing golf, he found many golfing friends at Oak Knoll, our municipal course. She said that some of the guys in the local men's golf club sort of adopted Patrick and filled some of the male roles in his life. She doesn't play golf but appreciates the friendly and caring people that are part of the golf community. Patrick is now 17.

When did you begin playing golf and what attracted you to the sport?

My grandfather bought me a set of golf clubs for Christmas when I was 12 years old. I always liked sports, so I thought I would try playing golf.

"Sometimes I feel I will sink the putt . . ." Oak Knoll Golf Course, Ashland, Oregon

Some of my middle school friends played golf, and I started playing with them and pretty soon I began playing a lot of golf. I really love the game and I played as much as I could. I especially liked playing with my friend Jesse, and he and I frequently played after school.

I never took any formal lessons, but I picked up the game from watching other golfers at the course, and some of my golfing friends at Oak Knoll gave me a few good tips. Sometimes I learned some good golf strategy from watching the golf channel. I practiced putting and chipping a lot at the local course.

I really like the challenge of golf and the good feeling I get when I hit a good shot. I try and copy all the mental and body feelings so that I know what it takes to make good ball contact. I love being in nature and walking around golf courses. I'm competitive, and I like to beat the people I play golf with. Competitiveness really keeps me going.

I love match play and the mental part of the game in "person-against-person" play. I really practice hard and like to win. I'm a high-school junior. I want to be involved professionally in golf as a career, and I hope I can get a college scholarship that will help me get started in that direction.

I like the feeling I have just knowing a shot is going to go in before I hit it. I feel the coolness of the air, the shadows in the late afternoon, and the overall calmness. I read the green. I sometimes feel I will sink the putt, and I do.

"And then the lover":

AND THEN THE LOVER

Golf, like a musical duet, was very popular during Victorian times because it was one way of being alone, unchaperoned, with someone of the opposite sex—a loaf of bread, a round of golf, and you. We've talked to couples young and old who prize the time they spend together alone on the fairways of dreams.

Christy Mabry and Darren Brogren

Christy has just graduated from college and loves golf. We talked to her and her boyfriend, Darren.

Christy, how did you get started?

Christy: My dad wanted a foursome to play with. My brother started. I said, "Hey, I want to play too." My mom gave us lessons to get us out of the house, away from the TV and to give us something to do during the summer. She would drop us off at the course and give us money. My dad didn't let us play on the course until we had practiced for a year.

Did Darren play before he met you?

No. I played 10 years by myself. Last year he expressed interest. We went to the driving range, and he liked it. I said, "You'll never play until you get some clubs."

Darren: I got some at a new-and-used sports store, and her dad gave me a putter. I won a golf bag at a beer convention.

Christy: We've been going together for almost two years. Golf's fun, relaxing. We enjoy the scenery and the company. (Laughs.) We treat every round as a practice round. He gets mad if I give him too much instruction.

I don't play by the usual rules. For example, I

don't take extra strokes for going into the water. It's enough that I've lost a ball. I played in tournaments, but people were way too serious. Those people aren't fun. It's fun for them, I suppose, but not for me.

Darren: You can talk to each other. If we go to a movie, you can't talk. With golf, it's the enjoyment of watching someone you like play. You think, "Wow, isn't that graceful."

Christy: Golf would be a really good first date. It would keep the focus off the uncomfortable emphasis on "both of us." You can always talk about golf. We play together all the time. His

twin brother is no fun because he likes to play by actual rules. I find out what my score is at the end of a round. Otherwise, I don't pay any attention.

Beth Hoffman
What has golf meant to you?

Mike and I used to live near Madison, Wisconsin, and our lives were very focused on two professional careers. We had the whole bit: two small children, a law practice, and running the financial business of a large corporation. We worked 60 to 80 hours every week. We didn't see each other very much during that time, and the children sometimes saw more of the nanny than of us.

Playing golf was one of the key things we did to stay in touch with each other during those hectic years. Every Friday afternoon (weather permitting), we would meet at the local golf course and play nine holes. We really connected on the course and enjoyed the time together without the burdens of work and parenthood.

Starting to sprinkle; who cares?

Just being together and walking the course helped us unwind and once again we discovered our "couple" relationship. Golf was a fun way to spend quality time together.

We frequently went out to dinner after playing golf, and this time was great because it allowed us to keep our focus on our relationship, our children, and the family. We talked about the kids, school, work stuff, and best of all, we "took care of us."

Robert and Jean Sheldon
How has golf been important to you?

Robert: We've played 50+ years as a couple or on our own. We organized an "Over-Par Golf Association." Once a year we would load up a cart with hors d'oeuvres and drinks and play a tournament. Eventually we attracted so many non-golfers that we had to give it up, but we had our tournaments for many years. Once it got so dark that one of our players had to light his cigarette lighter and put it in the hole so we could see to putt out. After the round, we would adjourn and go to a restaurant or have a barbecue.

The most important part was the social life and telling stories about lost balls and what happened out on the course. We've traveled to many countries to play, and we keep the scorecards. In Scotland, at the smaller courses, there is no pro. You go in, pick up a scorecard, deposit your money in a box, and go out and play. People in those countries play in all kinds of weather. We enjoy the game too much to let the weather bother us.

Jean: We enjoy the exercise and camaraderie. We had a group of eight couples that got together once a year. Some of us went to school together, and this was a chance to stay in touch. High and low handicappers played together for 36 years until age and infirmity raised their ugly heads. We had an old tin cup as a trophy. Bob and I retired that. One couple we know, the husband gave his wife a set of clubs for her 70th birthday. They played for a long time together.

Golden anniversary golfers

"Then a soldier."

THEN A SOLDIER

A number of golfers got their start in golf by playing on military courses. For them, golf provides rest and recreation, a team sport, and a home away from home. There are over 250 military courses in the United States and overseas on which they can play. When they leave the service or retire, they can continue to play on military courses. For them, the course becomes a place for reunions and inexpensive recreation.

Scott's brother, David, played golf when he was on active duty, so we talked to him about his Navy golf.

David English, the sailor
When did you begin playing and what attracted you to the game?

I started playing when I was about 15 years old. I went golfing with my cousin Jerry Jakubczak at the local Dunlop course in Buffalo, New York. We were both working at Jerry's Dairy Queen®, and two or three times a week we would get up at dawn and play 18 holes before opening the DQ at 11 a.m. I never took golf lessons, but my cousin gave me some helpful tips on the basics of the game. I loved the beauty of the early light, the companionship, and the peacefulness of golf at dawn. Those were two memorable and wonderful summers.

What can you tell our readers about Navy golf?

I didn't play golf again until I was 19 and had joined the Navy. I started playing in San Diego at the beautiful naval courses. It was relaxing and inexpensive recreation. I rented clubs and played with my buddies two or three times a month. I shipped out to Vietnam and the Philippines on an oiler. When I was at sea I really had fun hitting golf balls off the fan-tail of the ship. It was a great way to get a little exercise and work on my driving skills.

I frequently played at QB Point Golf Course in the Philippines—jungle golf. I really enjoyed the fresh air and exercise after spending two weeks working on a cramped ship. The course was very challenging due to the thick jungle vegetation and steep topography. The fourth hole was so steep that a rope tow was employed to help get up the hill to the plateau. The shot to the fifth hole, a sharp dogleg to the

Dancing on the green

etation was spectacular with amazing varieties, shapes, sweet fragrances, and a kaleidoscope of bright colors.

Any special golf moments that you would like to share?

One of my favorite golf outings occurred when I took my son Jonathon on vacation to the state of Washington. We played 27 holes of spectacular golf at the Ft. Lewis Golf Course. The course was park-like, with huge trees, colorful flowers, reflective ponds, and deep ravines. The green fees were only $8, which made it very affordable. My Navy retirement card was golden, as was the special time I spent with my teenage son.

right, was bordered by thick stands of tall bamboo poles.

Sometimes the golf shots that landed in the bamboo sounded like a billiard shot—bonk, bonk, bonk, bonk, and then silence. It was the land of no return for those shots.

What did you like about jungle golf?

I loved the colorful birds, mostly parrots, I think. There were also several kinds of monkeys that could be seen feeding on the wild figs that grew along the edges of the rough. The veg-

AND THEN THE JUSTICE

The age of the Justice is an age of wisdom. Maturity and experience mark this time of life. Golfers reflect about golf, friends made, memorable games played, places traveled, and stories and jokes told, heard, and laughed over.

Don English
How long have you been playing golf?

I started playing golf when I was in my 20s. I never took lessons, but I learned the basics of the game by watching other players. I was a regional sales manager for Jacuzzi Pumps®, and I serviced a six-state sales area which required a lot of travel time on the road. I frequently checked into a Holiday Inn® and made a reservation to play golf on a local course.

"And then, the justice"–

Playing golf was good exercise and my home away from home. I always met friendly people playing golf, which eased the loneliness of being far from home.

I was an avid golfer until I developed severe arthritis in my shoulder. The pain, discomfort, and loss of mobility made it impossible for me to play golf any longer. Golf used to be one of my life's joys, and I have some great memories of the games and people I met.

What are some of your favorite memories?

I was playing a course in Bohemia, New Jersey, with a salesman, and we joined another twosome to play a round of golf. I recognized the one guy because his picture was in the paper many times. He was the head of the Jersey Mafia. He seemed to be a decent sort of guy and quite friendly, but perhaps it's better not to mention his name.

On another occasion I was traveling in upstate New York, near Albany, and I checked into a motel in Poughkeepsie. It was around 2 p.m., so I asked the desk clerk where the nearest golf course was located. He made a few phone calls and lined up a tee time. I drove up the long, tree-lined lane of this beautiful course and entered a huge stone clubhouse.

I played golf with three men in their 50s. After the game they invited me for drinks and we shared some pleasant conversation about our

Uncle Don in the '50s, Island Hills Golf Course, Sayville, Long Island New York

game. As it turned out they were all judges, and the course was a private club for judges only. They treated me like a top-notch New York lawyer.

So the moral of these stories is you can meet all sorts of people on a golf course!

Barbara and Gloria Hiura
How did you get started?

Gloria: I got lessons so as not to be left out when my husband went golfing. At first I thought "What a silly game. Go around hitting a little ball." Later I decided to learn because I didn't always want to be left behind.

Then I gave my teenagers lessons, but they could have cared less about the game. My husband died, and I continued to play. Now my daughter and I play several times a week and take golfing vacations together.

Where have you been?

Barbara: Oh, we've gone to Europe, to Hawaii—anywhere we want to visit. We make sure there's golf.

Gloria: I've been to Scotland, Australia, and New Zealand with my daughter. Even Spain. On a course we played you can see the coasts of Africa and Europe.

How's your game?

Barbara: My mother, who's 76, hits straight. I can hit longer than she can, but she's always consistent. Just like a machine, always up and down in two, or so it seems. I didn't like playing with her when I was younger. I always wanted to beat her. But I like playing with her now.

What advice do you have for new players?

Barbara: Be patient. It's not an easy game to learn. You need lots of time. It's addictive. Don't you think it's addictive?

Gloria: Get lessons before you learn

A mother-daughter golfing vacation

mistakes that will haunt you and be very difficult to correct. Get lessons any time you need them. Otherwise, friends want to be helpful. They tell you to do this and that. You do this and that. Pretty soon your ball is going this way and that way and you have to unlearn all the this and that.

"The sixth age shifts"

THE SIXTH AGE SHIFTS

The sixth age is the "golden age." At this stage of life, golfers have reached their prime. Some of the people we spoke to have made significant contributions to their professions and some to the game of golf. Among their ranks were the visionaries and missionaries of social and political change. Their efforts opened golf to others. The following two interviews took place in Washington, D.C., at several municipal golf courses.

Ralph Glenmore
How did you start playing golf?

I'm now 72 years old. I'm the starter at the East Potomac Golf Course. I learned to play golf when I was around 15 at the Langston course in Washington, D.C. Clyde Martin, my uncle, was a black PGA professional, and he taught me the basics of the game. He also taught me how to shape shots, play strategic and competitive golf, and the importance of enjoying golf. Golf is a thinking man's game, and the game is played against yourself.

What can you tell us about the struggle of black people in their quest to play golf?

I have been playing golf for 60 years and have followed and participated in the social changes that now allow golf to be accessible to players of all color, race, gender, and age. I'm the grandson of Albert Martin, who was an African-American caddy master at the Congressional Country Club in Bethesda, Maryland, during the 1920s. He taught many black boys and men the art of caddying. In the process of learning how to caddy, many of them developed a sense of the game even though they were strictly forbidden to play golf during those times. Caddies were allowed only to carry the golf clubs of white golfers and were further restricted from utilizing golf equipment, practice areas, and other golf-related activities.

Ralph Glenmore (r.) and friend John Henderson
East Potomac Golf Course, Washington, D.C.

finding a hickory branch from the nearby woods that was then carved with a penknife to fit into the refurbished iron or wooden club head. The love of the game drove many of these early black golf pioneers into discovering unconventional and unique ways of playing the game.

How was the race barrier finally broken?

But some black caddies learned to play golf, right?

Many of the black caddies devised their own ways of playing the game. A common practice during these times was to sneak around to the wooded and secluded areas of the golf courses with the borrowed clubs of their white clients and play the game in secret. Moonlight, dusk, and dawn were favorite times for getting away to play a few holes with fellow caddies.

Sometimes they rescued the broken and discarded clubs of the white players from the trash heaps of the exclusive golf courses and repaired them to use in secret golf games. Oftentimes, the repair involved burning out the broken shaft and

Albert Martin, my grandfather, was instrumental in gathering support from the black community, white golfers, and influential people of that time to create the first golf course that black golfers could enjoy. Eleanor Roosevelt and the famous black civil rights leader, Senator John Mercer Langston, from Virginia, were two of the key persons during the early 1930s who finally convinced the decision-makers to establish a course on the site of an old garbage dump on the outskirts of Washington, D.C.

As a result of those early and sometimes heroic civil rights efforts, Langston public golf course was born in 1938. Finally, black Americans had a golf course they could claim as their own. The course was named after

Senator Langston, who was also the president of Howard University during the 1930s. The efforts of my grandfather and of those black golf players who followed him set the stage for the acceptance of players of all colors into the sport of golf.

Jimmy Garvin, General
Manager of Langston
Golf Course

Can you tell us how you began golfing?

I attended Howard University on a baseball scholarship and later I injured my arm while pitching and was unable to continue with my baseball career. I became interested in playing golf through my friend Chuck Hinton who played major league baseball for the Washington Senators and the Los Angeles Angels. Chuck was, and still is,

an avid golfer and became my mentor and golf teacher.

As a golf teacher and player, what suggestions can you give our readers?

I feel the values inherent in the golf game, such as respect for the game and your fellow players, good sportsmanship, appreciation of nature, and honesty are excellent life skills. I suggest being persistent and kick on doors if those doors are closed to your golf game aspirations. Love of the game will carry you through race barriers.

Does Langston provide any community outreach programs?

I have participated in several programs that are designed to introduce minority inner-city kids to golf. The kids get free golf lessons and donated equipment. We encourage them to learn

Jimmy Garvin (l) and Chuck Hinton, Langston Public Golf Course, Washington, D.C.

"Last scene of all"-

the game both as competitors and for the pure enjoyment. "Hook a Kid on Golf" and "Mason's Army" are two of the popular outreach programs offered at Langston. These programs also provide internships and neighborhood work opportunities for the kids.

LAST SCENE OF ALL

The last scene of all is the phase of life that we also refer to as the twilight years, a stage that includes golfers at life's end. It speaks volumes about a game that still counts the oldest generation as active players. These golfers have a wealth of experience and great "short game" skills.

Augie Hess
Tell us a bit about yourself.

I'm 86 years old, a Native American of the Paiute tribe, of the Mono Basin,

California. I have always been treated respectfully wherever I go. "The Big Guy" has always blessed me with a healthy body. I have no problems. My handicap is nine right now, but during the summer I usually play a seven or eight handicap.

Why do you play golf?

I just love the game. You play by yourself, figure out your next shot, which club to use, etc. I enjoy the camaraderie, meet a lot of nice people on the courses. Just being on the courses, which are usually beautiful and very challenging, makes you feel great, especially when you make good contact with your shots, and watch the ball go towards the greens. What a beautiful feeling!

How did you become interested in golf? What was your background?

When I was 48 years old, in 1963, I got membership in the Bishop Country Club, and really got involved in golf. I was a baseball player and that helped me a lot in learning how to play this game of golf. I had a lot of patience and tried to observe all the different shots that players with lower handicaps hit.

What advice would you give to beginning golfers?

Never took any lessons but I think a person starting to play golf should take lessons from a pro and learn all the fundamentals. Very important, then practice, practice. I got a shag bag which holds 75 to 80 golf balls, so every chance I got I would go down to a field near Mono Lake Park. Sheep men lease the property to graze sheep, and I found a great spot for hitting golf balls.

I marked out 100 yards, 150 yards, 200 yards, and 220 yards. So I used different irons for different lengths, and woods for longer shots. I would hit 75 to 80 balls, go pick them up with my shag bag, and do it all over again, until I got tired. Also, I would take my dog with me. She loves to go there to roam around. So in doing this I became a pretty good golfer.

Do you have any words of encouragement?

"Tee 'em high and let 'er fly!"

Art Koskella

This story is told by Steve Koskella, Art's son.

My father would die for a good game of golf and in the end, I think he did. Although his death makes me sad, given his choices, I think it was the way he wanted to go.

What was your father like?

My father was a large and powerful man. Even as an adult my thumb was about

the size of his little finger. He was a gentle person, though, and people tended to forget his physical prowess and any sense of intimidation as they got to know him.

The golf course was a good place for him. It brought out his qualities of controlled power mixed with gentleness, tenacity, and grace. He was quite an athlete. I heard stories of his being a basketball star in high school where he grew up in a tiny Finnish settlement in Long Valley, Idaho, a mile-high valley, where the winters were long and the snow was deep.

When did your dad begin playing golf?

He was a rancher and wrestled cattle, as well as hay bales and cranky farm machinery. He started golfing in his

Auggie Hess with his classic 1937 Cord at the Bishop Country Club, Bishop, California

50s, and I thought it was an old man's sport, though he played with guys my age and was always coming home with jackets and shoes and gift certificates he won at tournaments. I didn't realize that he was experiencing his magnificence out there, rocketing drives down the middle of the fairways, pitching balls

Courtesy Steve Koskella

Art in his Christmas golf sweater

on the greens with perfect control, and dropping putts like lead.

Did his game change?

I didn't play golf with him till he was in his 60s and had already had a total knee replacement. His back didn't give him much pain by then because the vertebrae formerly separated by worn-out discs had fused together. He still played 18 holes three times a week and brought home prizes. I could

never beat him till he reached his 80s.

By then he'd had his other knee replaced, which didn't turn out quite right. Worse yet, he had congestive heart failure and couldn't get his wind. I still remember the "whews" and the sweat as he struggled from the golf cart to the ball. He took to taking two clubs with him and used them as canes for support. His balance was shot and he would tend to tip over in his stance.

The amazing thing was that he could still hit the ball with incredible accuracy, confounding friends and relatives with a deadly short game that often gave him the lead even after taking a few extra strokes to get in range. I know it was a frustration for him, though. He had given up so much.

When did you last play with him?

The last time I played with him he did amazingly well for five holes, then he played out, and started missing shots. He refused to give up. It was spring and he was determined that he would get in shape for nine holes. On May 1, 1999, he had a good day. He worked out on his treadmill and stretching machine and mowed the lawn. That exertion probably cost him a few months of life, but it won him his dignity. That night he died in his sleep.

George Hannan

In May of 2000, George Hannan made a hole in one, his first ever, at the age of 95. His grandson, a stripling of

40, watched his grandfather tee off with a four-wood on the 108-yard hole, and then shouted, "Grandpa, you got a hole in one." The pro at the King's Valley Golf Course in Crescent City, California, where George plays told us that George refers to all the other golfers as "those kids."

How did you get started?

I was 65 when I started. My wife began playing golf, and she thought I should start. The next Christmas there were some clubs under the tree. I thought, "What am I going to do with those things?" I took some lessons, and now I play twice a week. I have a motorized caddy, so I can walk the course. I play twice a week, usually on the par-3, nine-hole course. But I can walk a par-72 course too.

What can you tell older people about the game?

It's a challenge. Some elderly people have nothing to do when they retire. I tell them to play golf. Have fun. You are not supposed to sweat over the score. You meet wonderful people. And golf is a walking game, unless your health won't let you walk, but then you can ride in a cart.

I like to see people that age get out and get the exercise. If they can

George "Hole-in-one" Hannan

Courtesy George Hannan

just get started, they will love it. Sometimes I just hate to see the 18th hole roll around. My son and his wife are too darned busy now to play. But I'm going to keep dinging at them until I get them back to the game.

GLOSSARY OF UNCOMMON GOLFING TERMS

(for those hard-to-describe golfing situations)

aquadextrous (a-kwa-**dex**-truss) *adj.* Able to land in water hazard equally well from right or left side of tee or fairway.

ballstalker (**ball**-staw-ker) *n.* Golfer who walks the edges of woods and roughs, searching out lost balls.

bugopia (bug-**oh**-pee-a) *n.* Visual defect causing golfer to focus on insect on ball or crossing line of putt.

curlyolis (kuhr-lee-**oh**-lis) *adj.* **effect** (i-fekt) *n.* Force acting on putt such that when ball should drop, its angular velocity is unexpectedly increased by earth's rotation, causing ball to come to rest directly behind cup without going in.

deadteebeat (ded-**tee**-beet) *n.* One who never repays borrowed tees. (See panteehandler.)

flaggression (fla-**gresh**-un) *n.* Any of variety of forceful on-the-green behaviors, such as rushing to grab flag, letting flag flap to distract person putting, and ramming pin into cup after putting poorly.

golful (**gaw**-ful) *adj.* Shot so bad, no one says anything for several moments after.

misanthrowp (mis-an-**throwp**) *v.* To attempt to hurl club farther than ball went.

panteehandler (**pan**-tee-hand-ler) *n.* One who continually requests tees from playing partners.

polygamic (po-li-**game**-ik) *adj.* Not really that tired at end of first round and ready to play another.

reriminations (re-rim-i-**nay**-shunz) *n.* Recurrent accusatory memories of putts that lipped cup but didn't fall.

rustigrastirt (ruhs-tee-**gras**-turt) *n.* 1) Composite material that collects in grooves of irons and bottom of golf bag; 2) golf club lint.

sandbiguous (sand-**big**-u-os) *adj.* Ball

lying in sand of such consistency player cannot easily choose club.

sinksure (**sink**-shoor) *adj.* Absolutely positive shot will go in before hitting it.

smughook (**smuhg**-uuk) *n.* Poorly executed shot sharply curving to left, caused by excessive pride in birdie on previous hole.

sticked off (stikt **off**) *adj.* coll. Feeling intense anger at ball's having hit pin and gone into sand bunker.

tanteelyze (**tan**-tee-lize) *v.* To leave behind chipped or broken tee in such position that person finding it thinks tee is whole and bends over to pick it up.

vereditgo (**hver**-dit-goh) *interrog. adv.* Confused, exclamatory question following shot golfer loses sight of.

yesitsin (**yes**-its-in; yes-**its**-in; yes-its-**in**) *interj.* Exclamation of confident delight that shot is going into cup. (Stress varies according to what stage of ball's flight or roll—initial, medial, terminal—golfer becomes convinced shot is good.)

BIBLIOGRAPHY

Baddiel, Sarah. *Beyond the Links: Golfing Stories, Collectibles, and Ephemera.* London: Studio Editions, 1992.

Baddiel, Sarah. *Golf: The Golden Years.* London: Bracken Books, 1989.

Bartlett, Michael, ed. *The Golf Book.* New York: Arbor House, 1980.

Barton, John and Hunki Yun. *Golf on the Web.* New York: MIS: Press, 1997.

Chambers, Marcia. *The Unplayable Lie: The Untold Story of Women and Discrimination in American Golf.* New York: Pocket Books, c1995.

Darwin, Bernard. *The Golfer's Companion.* London: J.M. Dent & Sons Ltd., 1937.

———. *Mostly Golf.* Ed. Peter Ryde. Stamford: Ailsa, 1986.

Frozen Foursome, The. *Golf on the Tundra.: The Official Rulebook of the Tundra Golf Association* J. Roseville, MN: Bad Dog Press, 1996.

Glenn, Rhonda. *The Illustrated History of Women's Golf.* Taylor Publishing Company: Dallas, 1991.

Golf: A Turn-of-the-Century Treasury. Secaucus, NJ: Book Sales Inc., 1986.

Graves, Robert Muir and Geoffrey S. Cornish. *Golf Course Design.* New York: J. Wiley, 1998.

Hogan, Ben and Herbert Warren Wind. *Five Lessons: The Modern Fundamentals of Golf.* New York: Barnes, 1957.

Liguori, Ann. *A Passion for Golf: Celebrity Musings About the Game.* Dallas: Taylor Publishing, 1997.

Linder, Mike. *Play It as It Lies: Golf and the Spiritual Life.* Louisville: Westminister John Knox Press, 1996.

Mann, Carol. *The 19th Hole: Favorite Golf Stories.* Stamford, CT: Longmeadow Press, 1992.

McCord. *The Golf Connoisseur: An Insider's Guide to Key Sources in the World of Golf.* New York: Lyons & Burford, 1996.

Murphy, Michael. *Golf in the Kingdom.* New York: Penguin Arkana, 1997.

Olman, John M. and Morton W. Olman. *Golf Antiques & Other Treasures of the Game.* Cincinnati: Market Street Press, 1997.

Peck, M. Scott. *Golf and the Spirit: Lessons for the Journey.* New York: Harmony Books, 1999.

Pressfield, Steven. *The Legend of Bagger Vance: Golf and the Game of Life.*

Avon Books, Inc., 1995.

Reilly, Rick. *Missing Links: A Novel*. New York: Doubleday, 1996.

Shoemaker, Fred and Pete Shoemaker. *Extraordinary Golf*. Berkeley: Berkeley Publishing Group, 1997.

Updike, John. *Golf Dreams: Writings on Golf*. New York: Knopf, 1996.

Valentine, Linda & Margie Hubbard. *Golf Games Within the Game: 200 Fun*

Ways Players Can Add Variety and Challenge to Their Game. New York: Perigee Books, 1987.

Wind, Herbert Warren, ed.. *The Complete Golfer*. New York: Simon and Schuster, 1954.

Wodehouse, P.G. *The Golf Omnibus*. New York: Random House, 1991.

INDEX